To: First Baptist ... ch
From: ...

19

50 STORIES TO CHALLENGE
YOUR FAITH AND INSPIRE YOUR SOUL

More Precious than Gold

COMPILED BY:
THE FAR EAST BROADCASTING CO. (PHILIPPINES), INC.

More Precious Than Gold
50 Stories to Inspire Your Faith and Challenge Your Soul
Compiled by FEBC Philippines

Scripture Quotations are from the Holy Bible,
New International Version unless otherwise indicated

ISBN. 971-92009-0-1

PRINTED BY DESIGN PLUS
QUEZON CITY, PHILIPPINES

To Our Great God and Savior
The Lord Jesus Christ
*who is the moving force
and guiding light behind
FEBC's 50 Years of Broadcasting
the Gospel by Radio*

Preface

*T*o see God's hand at work through 50 years of Gospel broadcasting calls for a celebration! A celebration of 50 years is a "Golden Anniversary" and so it is an honor and a privilege for us at FEBC Philippines to present this book "More Precious than Gold".

"More Precious than Gold" is also the theme for this year's Anniversary. Gold has often been called the most precious of metals. People have treasured it, saved up for it, lived for it and even died for it. But gold along with this earth will fade and lose its value in time.

What could be more precious than gold in God's sight than the billions of people living in this planet called earth? "For God so loved the world that He gave His one and only Son, that whoever believes in Him shall not perish but have eternal life" (John 3:16). Praise God for His tool of radio that can bring the Gospel to these millions of people who live in remote areas isolated from a church or in closed countries where open evangelism is prohibited. For the past 50 years, FEBC has been committed to the vision of bringing "Christ to the World by Radio".

For you who are not yet familiar with this ministry, FEBC is a non-profit, non-commercial international radio network that reaches out with the Gospel of Jesus Christ in more than 150 languages around the world. It began in the Philippines in 1948 and from the Philippines it broadcasts in more than 80 languages and dialects to the whole of Asia through 17 transmitters. Seven of these are used for international and ten for local broadcasting.

Included in these are both AM and FM stations in Metro Manila and regional stations throughout the Philippines.

This book is a testimony of God's goodness and saving grace in the lives of different people who have been touched by the broadcasts The stories represent the unseen millions who have been listeners of FEBC through the years and throughout the other parts of the globe. Some of the stories will make you smile or cry. Some will, hopefully, inspire your faith and help strengthen your walk with the Lord. Others will lift your soul in praise to God. Not only are these stories, also included are devotional insights at the end of each story.

You'll find stories that date as far back as 1948. Some are actual listeners' letters, first person accounts, while others have been rewritten for your reading pleasure. You will meet real people from all walks of life and different nationalities, people who have been touched by the Lord through radio. Perhaps you may even identify with one or two of them.

It is my prayer that as you read each story, you will be motivated to draw closer to our Lord Jesus Christ, you will be challenged to do your part for His Kingdom and you will invest your life and treasure in that which is truly "more precious than gold".

To you who have been a part of FEBC's ministry, thank you for your faithful partnership with us.

"SO FAITH COMES BY HEARING, AND HEARING BY THE WORD OF CHRIST. BUT I SAY, SURELY THEY HAVE NEVER HEARD, HAVE THEY? INDEED THEY HAVE:
'THEIR VOICE HAS GONE OUT INTO ALL THE EARTH, AND THEIR WORDS TO THE ENDS OF THE WORLD..'"   - (ROMANS 10:17-18)

TO GOD BE THE HONOR, GLORY AND PRAISE!

CARLOS L. PEÑA
President, FEBC Philippines

50th Anniversary, 1998

Table of Contents

Story 1

Journey to Forgiveness

*L*et's call her Susan. She requested that her real name not be published. A native of Negros, Susan was very happy that she received a scholarship for college because she belonged to a poor family and now her dream to finish her studies was coming to fruition.

However, that dream was short-lived for while Susan was still in her third year of high school, she was raped by an uncle. Since her family did not want any scandal, she was unable to do anything and justice was not served. To make matters worse, Susan was forced out of her house to live with another relative. Her grandmother, who was the mother of the one who raped her, spread vicious lies in her town, attacking Susan's person. Now the whole town was talking about her.

> *"Upon seeing her mother's dead body, Susan recounts that she lost all respect for her father. Hatred, bitterness and revenge were in her mind for what her father's family did."*

Shamed by the incident, Susan's mother fell ill and died. The next thing she knew, she was in front of her mother's coffin. Upon seeing her mother's dead body, Susan recounts that she lost all respect for her father. Hatred, bitterness and revenge were in her mind for what her father's family did.

Upon graduation from high school, Susan left for Manila to work in a drugstore. Her co-worker who was a Christian took her several times to church but this had no influence at all because all her thoughts were full of revenge.

One day, however, this co-worker turned on her radio to DZAS. The program at that time was a drama called *"Tanikalang Lagot"* (Unshackled). The story of the Christian being featured moved her to tears and for the first time, Susan realized that Jesus Christ was the only one who could change her heart and life. And so at that moment, she asked the Lord into her life and asked Him to change her. "My heart that was full of anger and hatred was replaced with a heart of understanding. The Lord removed all my thoughts of revenge and He reminded me that vengeance is His. Now peace floods my heart," she testifies.

Susan continues to listen to DZAS and has found the counseling program **Heartline** helpful in relating to her family, particularly her brothers and sisters. Songs that she listens to minister to her. She cannot help but praise and thank the Lord for using DZAS to introduce her to Christ and the new life He offers.

FORGIVENESS- HOW WE ALL NEED IT! WE HAVE FREELY RECEIVED IT FROM GOD BUT IT CAN ALSO BE DIFFICULT TO FREELY GIVE TO THE ONE WHO HAS WRONGED US. WE FEEL WE HAVE THE RIGHT TO WITHHOLD FORGIVENESS BECAUSE WE WERE UNJUSTLY TREATED AND THIS HAS CAUSED A LOT OF HURT AND BITTERNESS. BUT IF CHRIST DID NOT FREELY FORGIVE US FOR THE WRONGS WE HAVE SO DESERVED, WHERE WOULD WE BE? IS THERE ANYONE FROM WHOM YOU ARE WITHHOLDING FORGIVENESS?

Verse: *"Be kind and compassionate to one another, forgiving each other, just as in Christ God forgave you."* (EPHESIANS 4:32)

The Amazing Talking Box and a Village

" Long ago Fua Tai, the supreme god who created all things, lived and mingled among his people. They had a good relationship. But one day, the harmony between man and god was shattered. Fua Tai was offended, repulsed by his people's behavior that he abandoned them to the spirit world. From then on, the evil spirits disciplined and punished the people."

- HMONG FOLKLORE

*T*he Hmong people of Laos are simple villagers who tend and harvest crops, who love music and feasting. Every night, after a day's work, they would sit around campfires and listen to their elders tell stories about Fua Tai and the spirits.

The Hmong were animists -- spirit worshippers. They believed evil spirits were everywhere…in trees, rocks and rivers… hounding and bringing them suffering and pain. They offered sacrifices and drank blood to appease the spirits while continuing to live in fear and bondage.

However, something unusual happened - 23 years ago in a remote Hmong village in the jungle mountains of Northern Laos.

A "talking box" became the center of interest among the village people. They gathered around to listen to a peculiar message that they could easily understand. The story they heard aroused their interest, for it was totally different from the tales told by their elders. It told of someone who loved and saved people and did not abandon them. It was a story of hope and security in God, not fear from the evil spirits.

"Who could this god be?" they asked. They had to find out!

The voice on the box told them to respond to a post office box in the capital city of Vientiane. To the simple Hmong, the answer was obvious: He must be at that post office box address. The village elders appointed three men to make the long trip to the city. Somehow, they found the post office and there, they waited. Three days later, they saw a man who came to pick up his mail. They asked him if he was the supreme god. The man assured them that he was not... but that he could help them know God.

Hmong people listening to the broadcasts in their church in North Vietnam.

The man went to the Hmong village and told them about God. He told them of His plan from the very beginning and how He wanted to have fellowship with them. He told them too that it was not God who left the people, but it was the people who left Him because they sinned. But though they sinned, God loved them so much that He gave His only Son Jesus, that all who believed in Him will be restored to that fellowship.

There, deep in the jungle, it was like the second day of Pentecost! Around 3,000 people left the dark world of spirit worship for a new life and light in Jesus Christ.

In 1991, startling information appeared in a Hanoi Sunday newspaper which referred to an apparent Christianization of the Hmong of the Vietnam highlands. The article blamed specific messages in radio broadcasts from Manila for this mass conversion. While subsequent articles made further references to the phenomenon, it was only in 1993 that the first communication was received from the Vietnamese Hmong themselves, which presented a "census" of believers... 330,000 Christians! Recent (1997) contact with the Vietnamese Minority Affairs officials has confirmed that the government assesses the number of Christians to be around 250,000.

Here is a letter from a Hmong listener in North Vietnam:

"The village that I am currently in has 150 Christian families. We have regular services but at different places. This year the Vietnamese government has tried to close off all of our churches. They have interrogated our faith and threatened punishment on our behalf. What should we do? Please request prayer for our people. We pray that whatever happens to us, we will not fade away from Him.

Your radio broadcast has really helped us all to walk with the Lord. We thank God that by faith through Jesus Christ we all know each other. Remember that we have no pastor and we depend only on what the radio has to say about God. May God give you strength and wisdom from above so that you may continue bringing the Gospel to us."

THE WORD OF GOD IS POWERFUL TO FREE PEOPLE FROM THE EVIL THAT BINDS THEM. AS WE TAKE THE AUTHORITY THAT THE LORD HAS GIVEN US TO SPEAK FORTH HIS WORD AND HIS NAME, THE WORKS OF THE DEVIL WILL CRUMBLE. VICTORY IS OURS NOT ON THE BASIS OF OUR FLESH, BUT IN THE MATCHLESS NAME OF OUR GREAT GOD AND SAVIOR JESUS CHRIST - GLORY TO HIS NAME! WHAT SITUATIONS IN YOUR LIFE HAVE YOU USED TO PROCLAIM CHRIST'S NAME TO HELP SET OTHERS FREE FROM SIN?

Verse: *"That at the name of Jesus every knee should bow in heaven and on earth and under the earth, and every tongue confess that Jesus Christ is Lord to the glory of God the Father."* - (PHILIPPIANS 2:10-11)

Tortured for Christ in Saudi Arabia

*D*onnie Lama had been working in Saudi Arabia since 1984 as an Overseas Contract Worker. Through the years, he was able to build a good track record, after being cited by his employer as "most outstanding employee". In October 1995, he returned to Saudi Arabia after a vacation in the Philippines.

Donnie Lama heard about the broadcasts while he was in a Saudi Arabian prison.

It was 5:00 p.m. and Donnie was talking to a fellow employee on the telephone at his place regarding something unusual that happened the previous night. Several Muslim police authorities had come at 11:00 p.m. until 1:00 a.m. trying to force open their door. He and his companion hid in their room praying. They also hid all their Bibles, cassette tapes and other Christian items. The entry was unsuccessful but the police returned that afternoon and Donnie unknowingly opened the door after a knock and he was immediately handcuffed and strangled.

"What's the problem?" Donnie asked. They said ,"You come with us. You are the problem." Donnie did not know why he was being arrested. He was locked up with another prisoner in an isolation cell that could only accommodate one. The two weeks that followed were never to be forgotten.

Every night guards would pull him out for interrogation. They were forcing him to admit to the crime of murder which he never committed. Donnie suffered excessive physical and verbal abuse during that time -- he was kicked, slapped, beaten and spat on for hours on end.

The police were unable to make him admit to his crime so he was charged with "being a preacher of Christianity". During the raid at his home, they found an old photograph of him taken in 1984 speaking before a group in a church setting. Prior to this, Donnie had been active in the underground church. This photo was used as evidence against him and so he was subjected to even greater cruelty by his interrogators. He was later transferred to Al Malaz prison in Riyadh, the largest and most notorious in Saudi Arabia.

Along with two fellow accused, Donnie suffered mental torture together with physical battery. They were locked up in a three by four meter cell with a madman who was imprisoned for murdering his brother. Peace and sleep were far from them as they lived with this man who could attack them anytime. The guards were cruel and barely gave them edible food.

In the jail, however, Donnie found the radio to be his source of comfort and peace. He would listen to the program *Kumusta Po Kabayan* produced by FEBC Philippines aimed at Filipinos living in the Middle East. Donnie relates: *"Sometimes the broadcast signal would be weak so I would keep the radio very near my ears. I would go to different parts of the cell to get good feedback. I was truly encouraged spiritually through the program. It really strengthened me throughout all my persecutions. The Word of God was my strength and the program was so alive for me."* Donnie would gather his co-inmates and they would listen together.

Donnie thought of writing Pastor Ed Lapiz, speaker in the program. He would always hear Pastor Lapiz say, "For those of you who are in jail- we are praying for you. These are the words of God so you can be strengthened."

How was Donnie released? He tells us that God helped them find a way to send letters to those outside. Along with the other Filipino prisoners, they would roll their letters tightly and insert them in the drinking straws that came with their drinks. Here is a portion of his letter to FEBC Philippines while he was in jail:

"It has been nearly ten months now that I've been in this Al Malaz Jail in Saudi Arabia. If I had not been in jail, I would not have learned about your radio program. I have never stopped listening to it. It is very difficult for us to send out any note from here. Aside from the physical torture, our minds are tortured as well with worries and homesickness. My only hope is that our dear Lord will not forsake me and open the eyes of the Saudi authorities to pardon me for my aim is only to serve God. Pray for me and my fellow inmates to be released soon and be united with our families"

Through the prayers of people like those in FEBC, the letters of other Christians around the world and the intervention of the ministry of Open Doors and foreign embassies, Donnie Lama was released a year and a half later after having received 70 lashes on his body. While he was being lashed, he said: "Lord I offer you the 70 lashes in the same way that you received yours while you were here on earth."

Today Donnie lives in Cavite but he will not forget how the Lord never abandoned him during the most difficult time of his life. During an interview at FEBC, he says this to those who are experiencing trials: "Whatever trials you are facing, give your life to the Lord because it is only He who can help you and strengthen your faith. Look to Him alone and He will give you strength. Don't lose hope and keep praying to our Lord."

HOW MANY OF US WOULD CONTINUE IN THE FAITH IF WE SUFFERED PERSECUTION, EVEN IMPRISONMENT? WOULD WE GIVE IN AND DENY OUR LORD JESUS CHRIST? PRAISE GOD THAT THROUGH RADIO, GOD MINISTERED TO THIS BROTHER EVEN IN JAIL, ENABLING HIS FAITH TO BE STRENGTHENED. HOW FAITHFUL WILL GOD FIND YOU IN SPITE OF ALL THE TRIALS THAT COME YOUR WAY?

Verse: *"Do not be afraid of what you are about to suffer. I tell you, the devil will put some of you in prison to test you; and you will suffer persecution...Be faithful even to the point of death and I will give you the crown of life".* (REVELATION 2:10)

No Disability in God's Service

I am Reynold Malinao, second of nine children. My family is from Naujan, Oriental Mindoro in the Philippines. My father is a contractual laborer in a coconut plantation. Off season he finds work as a farm weeder. When he really can't find work my mother's income as a laundry woman helps foot the bill.

I was fifteen years old when I stopped going to school because of deteriorating vision. Doctors in our province could not find the cause. When I became blind on both eyes I was advised to go to Manila because according to them I could undergo an operation that will help me regain my sight. But when I came to Manila, it was learned that a tumor in my brain caused my blindness and that an operation is a must to stop the tumor from harming my body. If not taken immediately I have a slim chance of living up to a year. But my parents and I decided against it. We were thinking, what is the use of an operation if it will not help me see again?

"But when I came to Manila, it was learned that a tumor in my brain caused my blindness and that an operation is a must to stop the tumor from harming my body."

My situation was hard for my family. They were hurt. They were depending on me to help the family earn a living. My mother kept crying, asking why it had to happen when I was the healthy one, the one who could support our family. Questions I had no answer for. I started to listen to the radio to amuse myself.

One day I turned the radio dial to a program called *Tanglaw sa Landas ng Buhay* (Guide for Life's Path), on a station called DZAS. I started to listen and liked what I was hearing. This is where I first heard that God had a plan for me, that each person should have hope in his life. I began to have hope. Because of this I never blamed anyone for what happened to me. I developed strength. I became bold enough to venture outside the house. I taught myself how to walk in and out of our house by myself.

On December 26, 1992 while listening to DZAS, God enlightened me that hope in my heart was not enough. I need Jesus in my life because He is the bringer of hope. I immediately decided to welcome Him in my life.

Reynold Malinao, a blind listener, shared his testimony of salvation through the programs of DZAS

After that day, my life changed for the better. I used to be bored for lack of things to do but I started to have peace in my day to day life. There is joy in my heart even though I cannot see. My family had a hard time understanding my change of faith but when they saw my happiness and the change in my life, they finally accepted my decision.

An OMF missionary went to Manila to get Bibles for me from the office of Resources for the Blind, Inc. (RBI). Her visit opened the way for me to get into a Bible School.

I am happy at Wesleyan Bible College because this is what my heart desires. I did not have problems in adjusting with my classmates because the best gift that the Lord gave me is love. Love for others. No matter who or what they are. I pray that I may able to finish my studies. That is why I am doing my best. I hope to share the Word or become a pastor as my ministry after school.

Oh! And about my brain tumor? It's almost five years now and I do not feel anything. I feel strong and healthy. I am even gaining weight. I thank God for this.

MANY PEOPLE LIVE IN DARKNESS— NOT PHYSICAL BUT SPIRITUAL DARKNESS. BECAUSE OF SIN, MAN HAS BECOME SEPARATED FROM A HOLY AND RIGHTEOUS GOD. SPIRITUAL DARKNESS CAN BE MORE FRIGHTENING THAN HAVING NO EYESIGHT FOR ITS CONSEQUENCES ARE ETERNAL. THOSE WHO ARE SAVED WILL HAVE THEIR BLIND EYES OPENED IN HEAVEN AND THEY SHALL BEHOLD THE FACE OF THEIR SAVIOR WHO IS THE LIGHT OF THE WORLD.

Verse: *" I am the light of the world. Whoever follows me will never walk in darkness but will have the light of life."* (JOHN 8:12)

I Left Russia

*M*r. Eugene Bresenden was a listener to Christian broadcasts for many years. He and his family have come out of Russia by a miracle of God. He worked as FEBC's Russian broadcasting consultant, with a burning desire to set his people free. He says, " I want the free world to know the truth about the Christians inside Russia. I want my people to sleep without the continual fear of 'the knock' on their door and the voice 'Open up! We have come for your child!'" Here is his story:

Knock-Knock! Knock!

"Open up! Secret Police!"

"Mother, mother, "I shouted in a loud whisper - "S-E-C-R-E-T P-O-L-I-C-E."

It was one o'clock in the morning. My heart began to pound as I remembered the threat mother had got: "Your son will be taken and you will go to prison if you don't stop teaching the Bible."

Mother slowly opened the door.

"Mrs. Bresenden!" one of them yelled.

The five men knocked her aside and began a two-hour ransacking of our home. I remember well the overturned tables, everything we owned thrown in the middle of the floor. Under the flooring, in the attic -- not a square inch was missed in their search.

Then they took mother off into the night -- I was 8 and she was 29 years old. Father had been killed in the army, so only grandmother and I were left.

Mother was tried, convicted and sentenced to 10 years in a slave labor camp in Northern Siberia. She spent much of her prison term pushing wheelbarrows full of heavy rocks. Roads were needed and slave labor camp cheap. The inhuman guards would often make mother and the rest of the prisoners lie down in the icy water until they were numb and half frozen. Then they would have to run with loaded wheelbarrows to keep from freezing to death. It was only mother's strong faith in God and her prayers for me that kept her alive.

Shortly after mother was taken, "the knock" again came on our door. This time it was for me. With my "wicked mother" gone, they wanted me to be brought up right - in a state orphanage.

While there I was watched closely. They made me believe my mother was a very wicked criminal. I was brainwashed day after day in atheistic communism until I believed as they did.

"My heart began to pound as I remembered the threat mother had got: "Your son will be taken and you will go to prison if you don't stop teaching the Bible."

Six years passed. Mother was released from prison and I was released from the orphanage, a converted communist and atheist.

The first day back home I tried hard to convince my mother and other Christians there was no God. "He is a dream of your mind," I would tell them. But they just kept on praying.

It was just a short time until mother's prayers were answered and I accepted Christ at age 14. I became active in youth work in the underground church. There I heard about Christian radio programs coming from the Far East and became a regular listener. My faith in

Christ was strengthened as I listened night after night to Jack Koziol from FEBC Manila.

Then at age 21 "the knock" again was for me. I was tried, convicted and sentenced to three years in a Siberian labor prison. The three years were filled with long hours of hard work, but God was with me.

I was released and again got back into the underground church, only this time in a bigger way. I traveled extensively across Russia, visiting many church leaders, distributing Bibles and learning more and more about religious oppression of my Russian people.

I learned that Russia had concurred to allow freedom of religion as stated in the United Nations and Helsinki Agreements. The communists want the outside world to believe this freedom is a reality.

I found that the continual threat of having one's children taken away if they are taught religion is not only true in many parts of Russia, but a fearful threat to all. The Christians are used for slave labor, their children are taken from them and, worse than being thrown in the river, as were the children of Israel, they are thrown to the atheists for their spiritual death.

THE CHILDREN WHOM THE LORD HAS GIVEN TO US ARE PRECIOUS IN HIS SIGHT. IT IS NOT ONLY A PRIVILEGE TO HAVE THEM IN OUR CARE BUT A RESPONSIBILITY TO TEACH AND TRAIN THEM IN THE FEAR OF THE LORD. NO INSTITUTION SHOULD TAKE OVER THIS RESPONSIBILITY WHICH WAS GIVEN TO PARENTS. PRAISE GOD FOR THE FREEDOM WE HAVE IN OUR COUNTRY TO NURTURE AND TEACH THE LITTLE ONES AT HOME. ARE YOU FULFILLING YOUR GOD-GIVEN RESPONSIBILITIES TOWARD THE CHILDREN ENTRUSTED TO YOU?

Verse: "*Fathers, do not exasperate your children, instead, bring them up in the training and instruction of the Lord.*" (EPHESIANS 6:4)

A Warning to Those Who Forget

"People who want to get rich fall into temptation and a trap and into many foolish and harmful desires that plunge them into ruin and destruction. For the love of money is the root of all kinds of evil. Some people, eager for money, have wandered from the faith and pierced themselves with many griefs." (I TIMOTHY 6:9-10)

he words of this Bible passage cut at the heart of Mel and Ruth Torriana. They knew it was God speaking directly to them through the radio program **Heartline**. The topic for the week- "The Love of Money." Why did the message have such an impact in their lives? Why did they cry out to God in agony, tears and repentance as they heard the counselor talk about the love of money being the root of all evil?

Let's backtrack and listen to their story which they wrote to FEBC last February 23, 1998:

"We were married in 1993, having had a previous experience of salvation in the Lord Jesus Christ. We were actively serving the Lord in our church. Our means of livelihood came from farming and raising pigs. We were faithful to the Lord and so He granted us a prosperous life. However, there came a time when we were no longer satisfied with what we had been earning and desired to have a more prosperous lifestyle. In so doing, my husband had to work longer hours, even on Sundays which were to be set apart for the Lord. He reasoned out that the Lord would always understand him. He also ran for office in the *baranggay* (village). He would charge 10% interest per month over all those who borrowed money from him and two cavans palay (rice seed) profit for every P1,000 lent per cropping season until it became common business practice.

We got the lifestyle that we had wanted. We had more money -- not through the means the Lord wanted but through our own ways.

"We went to so many doctors even in Manila and found that no one could cure him. Almost all our money was spent because of his sickness. The sixth doctor who diagnosed him told my husband to undergo an AIDS test."

However because of all this, my husband seldom went to church and his time with our family was diminished. He was busy with other things that he forgot to pray to the Lord. That is why in the midst of all this God allowed him to have a sickness that bothered him for over two years. He developed itchiness in various parts of his body and along with this his mouth, lips, tongue and gums were afflicted with so many sores that contained pus and blood. Because of this, he wasn't able to speak clearly and could only take soup as his food.

We went to so many doctors even in Manila and found that no one could cure him. Almost all our money was spent because of his sickness. The sixth doctor who diagnosed him told my husband to undergo an AIDS test. We could not accept having to undergo such test because he had always been a faithful husband and had never received a blood transfusion in his life. It was the first time I saw my husband cry.

On the day we were about to go to Manila for the AIDS test, I tuned in to your radio program **Heartline** on DZAS and God used it to speak to us and show us our sin. The topic that day was "The Love of Money" and I Timothy 6:9-10 was being discussed. There were several callers on the phone who were asking for advice regarding their business of loaning money to receive 5% profit per month. It really struck me that we were even asking for 10%. As soon as my husband arrived, I shared to him what I heard on the radio. Together we asked the Lord's forgiveness , we repented and told Him that we would leave such a dishonoring form of business.

Together with our church members, we prayed and fasted, seeking the Lord's help and in one week all of my husband's sores and sickness were gone without the use of any medicine- Praise the Lord! God is indeed faithful. We did not go to Manila for the AIDS test anymore. He had been healed. God is our Jehovah Rapha!"

THE LORD'S DISCIPLINE IS MORE OFTEN THAN NOT PAINFUL. HE MAY BRING SICKNESS OR SOME TRIAL IN LIFE TO CONFRONT US WITH OUR SINFULNESS. IT IS DURING THOSE TIMES OF TRIAL THAT WE SHOULD RESPOND NOT WITH BITTERNESS BUT WITH AN OBEDIENT AND REPENTANT HEART. IN SO DOING, CLEANSING WILL FOLLOW AS WE ARE RESTORED TO A RIGHT FELLOWSHIP WITH HIM. HOW ARE YOU RESPONDING TO THE TRIALS THAT GOD IS SENDING YOUR WAY?

Verse: *"It is good for me that I was afflicted, that I may learn Thy statutes"* (PSALM 119:71- NASB)

A Child Shall Lead Them

Story 7

*T*he night had been dark and long for Kuta. As in other nights, he could not sleep for he was anxious because his father had told his mother days before that he would have to join him at work in the rubber plantations. He thought about how much he would miss his mother, leave his world of childhood and enter a new world. Kuta and his family live on the large beautiful island of Sumatra in Indonesia where majority of the people embrace the Muslim faith.

Kuta was afraid because he knew that his father would treat him just as other Muslim fathers in Indonesia treat their sons. He would treat him as though he were worthless. Boys had to earn their fathers' respect and that was not easy.

Sure enough Kuta's father returned for him the next day. It would be his first day to work in the field but he was not excited. "Things will not be the same for you now, Kuta. You must always follow your father and never question him no matter how lowly and dirty the work," his mother said. "Go with your father and someday make him proud of you." So off Kuta went to begin a new life. In a few weeks, he got used to the path that led from their home to the rubber plantation. He got used to working with the men for long hours under the hot sun.

Kuta had an older sister named Sunali but now that he was a "man," he was allowed to shout at her and boss her around. She would wash his feet along with their father's each time they arrived from the field. But Kuta, still a child at heart, would still play and share secrets with his favorite sister.

The biggest secret that Kuta and Sunali shared was the radio programs they heard each evening from FEBC Philippines. Every evening when their father was busy with his friends talking and smoking, Kuta and his sister

An Indonesian boy, similar to Kuta, keeps tuned to the broadcast even as he goes to the fields on his carabao.

would quietly slip away to their vegetable garden and there, hiding behind the corn, would tune in to this station coming from the Philippines. They were afraid to turn the volume up lest they be found out. Night after night they tuned in to listen to the message that spoke to their hearts -- the message about a God who loved them enough to send His Son Jesus to die for them and forgive their sin. Kuta and Sunali did not talk much about what they heard over the radio, but they did think about it specially before they went to sleep.

One afternoon, Kuta noticed a tear drop from Sunali's eyes. She dried them very quickly and continued her household duties. Kuta could tell something was bothering her. That night as together they sat huddled around the radio Sunali said: "Kuta, I believe what these people on the radio are saying." Kuta told her, "Father won't allow it. You are not going to tell anyone and we will not speak of it again." he said in a sad voice.

As weeks passed, Kuta noticed a change in his sister's behavior. He saw how joyful and peaceful she was. She became gentle and helpful in a way that Kuta did not see in other Muslim women. One night as once more they were listening to the radio program, they heard one of their younger brothers shouting   they had been found out!

"What are you two doing?" one of the boys said. Before Kuta could change the station, his brother snatched the radio from his hands and brought it into his house turning up the volume. Kuta and his sister were frightened. What could they do now?

Kuta's father appeared at the doorway and asked who had been taking the radio out of the house. Kuta replied trembling, "We...I've been listening to the broadcasts coming from FEBC Philippines. And I believe that Jesus is the Christ and not Mohammed." Everyone in the house seemed frozen at the spot. At that instant his father grabbed him and with a thin bamboo pole beat him mercilessly to the ground until blood ran down his face. Kuta's mother came screaming, begging him to stop. She stepped between them to save his life.

At last after nearly killing his son, Kuta's father said to his mother, "Bandage his wounds and send him away in the morning. I never want to see him again!"

The next morning, Kuta set out to go to his uncle's place in Jakarta. After a week of traveling on foot, he finally reached the place. Kuta didn't understand what happened but there was a peace in his heart that God would take care of him. He now belonged to the Savior and he found the joy he had been looking for in spite of his being away from his family. God provided for Kuta as he worked in several small jobs. He was even able to save enough money to send to FEBC Philippines to ask for a Bible. Each moment was precious as he read it.

A friend saw him with a Bible and introduced him to some people he knew. He began to work for this Christian family and grew in his faith and knowledge in the Word. Kuta was now twenty years old. The Christian family took an interest in Kuta and gave him money to visit his family. On each visit Kuta would share to his five brothers the Word of God until one by one they received Jesus Christ into their lives. But it became more difficult to talk to his parents as they saw their children leave Islam. They were very bitter against Kuta.

The years sped by and the Christian family with whom he was staying found Kuta to be a dedicated Christian. They decided to pay for his studies in a Bible School until eventually Kuta was pastoring a church.

It wasn't long before Kuta received word that his brother Manwali was dying and in the hospital. He immediately went to him and as he saw his brother, his parents arrived. They did not want to visit their Christian son but then changed their minds. Manwali pled with his parents that they receive Jesus as their Savior. "Don't hold on to your sin any longer. How happy I would be to see you before I die and know that you would give your hearts to Jesus". To everyone's amazement, their parents, with tears in their eyes, knelt by his deathbed and accepted Jesus into their hearts. The whole family had finally come to Christ. Kuta's prayers were answered as Manwali went on peacefully into God's presence.

THE LORD DOES NOT LOOK AT AGE OR STATUS TO SEE WHOM HE WOULD CHOOSE FOR HIS KINGDOM. EVEN CHILDREN , AS THEY COME IN FAITH, CAN EXPERIENCE HIS GRACE AND RENEWING POWER. THE CHILD HAS HIS WHOLE LIFE BEFORE HIM TO SERVE THE LORD, ONCE HE HAS COME TO KNOW CHRIST AS SAVIOR. LOOK AT THE CHILDREN AROUND YOU AND THINK- WHAT CAN I DO TO HELP THEM KNOW CHRIST AND GROW IN HIM?

Verse: *"And He said, 'I tell you the truth, unless you change and become like little children, you will never enter the kingdom of heaven. And whoever welcomes a little child like this in my name welcomes Me".*
(MATTHEW 18:3,5)

Instrument of Noble Purpose

*G*loom and sadness marked Aida's life. Poverty and a broken home welcomed her arrival to the world. It did not seem enough to have such somber atmosphere grace her birth; she herself was a picture of a dejected, hopeless creature.

Aida grew up with her four sisters and brothers amidst destitution and want. Her father, a brutal man and usually drunk, would come home bringing more trouble to his family. Aida's mother suffered physical and mental torture from her husband.

Here is Aida Purificacion writing with her foot, proving to us that God can still use His vessels no matter how weak.

The father lived from day to day for drinking, gambling and womanizing until finally, he left his family for another woman. Mrs. Purificacion was left to shoulder the responsibilities of a mother and father. She had to work double time in various odd jobs to raise her children as decently as she could. Trying hard to make both ends meet to feed five children, her health gradually deteriorated.

Her weakened body, however, did not survive for long the heavy burden of raising a family all by herself. When Aida was one year old, Mrs. Purificacion died, leaving the children behind in the care of their grandmother.

Aida was born severely deformed, her arms completely useless. Her limp legs were not strong enough to carry her weight so she moved about by crawling or by being pushed on a wheelchair. Her young life was miserable, especially as she saw the seeming injustice and unfairness around her. While other girls her age enjoyed their health and youth, she mourned her frail, imperfect body.

Dark clouds, however, do not remain in the skies forever. One day while listening to her radio, Aida tuned in to DZAS. A Tagalog program powerfully impressed the message of God's love in her heart. There was an invitation to come to Jesus and she prayed with the broadcaster and received Christ as Savior and Lord of her life.

Joy, peace and love were meaningless words to Aida until Jesus Christ came into her life. She now testifies of her faith strongly. Using her foot, she wrote FEBC saying,

I am grateful to God for the faith which He planted in my heart. It is this faith which motivated me to develop the talents He gave me. I only learned how to read and write the A-B-C and that's all. But look at me now, I can write and draw with my foot very well. I even embroider with my feet. And, you know, all these talents and everything I have I gladly offer to my Savior.

Aida is determined to use the talents she has for the glory of her Savior whom she dearly loves. Now, her days count meaningfully for the God she serves through the little things she can do for others. Today, she's a glowing witness for Jesus in spite of her frail body and delicate health. Her constant companion is her radio from where she continues to get lessons and directions in the Christian life.

FOR SOME PEOPLE LIFE IS FILLED WITH "IF ONLY'S"—"IF ONLY I HAD MORE MONEY," "IF ONLY I LIVED IN A BIGGER HOUSE," "IF ONLY I LOOKED PRETTIER." BUT GOD WILL NOT ALLOW US TO DWELL IN THE PAST LEST WE WALLOW IN SELF-PITY. HE MAY NOT CHANGE OUR CIRCUMSTANCES BECAUSE HE WANTS US TO SEE THAT HE CAN TAKE WHATEVER CIRCUMSTANCES TO BRING ABOUT HIS PURPOSES AND THUS ENABLE US TO LIVE A MEANINGFUL LIFE.

Verse: *"And we know that in all things God works for the good of those who love Him, who have been called according to His purpose".*
(ROMANS 8:28)

Exiled in Siberia

*I*n 1969, a young Soviet man named Boris (not his real name) came across the radio broadcasts from FEBC Philippines' transmissions. Through the "electronic encounters," Boris was powerfully converted to Jesus Christ. But really there are no chance encounters when it comes to Christian radio -- these are divine appointments arranged by the Holy Spirit. After finding Christ, Boris sought to lead his wife to the Lord.

In prison he was not only repeatedly physically abused, but he was also given injections and forced to take mind - bending drugs.

This young man began writing FEBC Manila requesting a Bible and Christian literature. These were sent to him soon after. The KGB intercepted the package and he was reported to the authorities for witnessing to his wife. This resulted in his arrest and his being sent to a "psychiatric prison" in Siberia where he spent the next 20 years!

In prison he was not only repeatedly physically abused (Boris now has no teeth left and a broken arm which wasn't properly set), but he was also given injections and forced to take mind - bending drugs.

Occasionally, he was able to hear radio broadcasts which helped to strengthen his faith.

Many years later, Boris was released. He now lives in restricted exile on a small island off the frozen coast of Siberia, an area he describes as "where the white bears live." While there, he once again wrote asking for a Bible and Christian materials. These have helped him in his spiritual growth and he has occasional fellowship with other Christians.

Boris was a brand new Christian when he was sent to the psycho-prison where he underwent terrible tortures. How did his new-found faith survive those 20 years!? Some quotes from his letters will tell you:

"I had such a deep conversion and belief in Christ with the whole of my being and soul that I renounced all knowledge which is not necessary for mankind as strange."

"Behind all of this knowledge stands the devil to distract man from the Truth. It is a slippery road. I went through it all....it was a strange path! It was not my choice. All of this worldly knowledge of the cosmos did not bring me to an understanding of God."

"I am very thankful to you. We (Soviets) were lost in the darkness. They took God from us. You cannot understand how terrifying it is when you are stripped of all spiritual values. This is frightful, I experienced all of it."

God has now placed a deep spiritual burden on this man, living in exile, on Sakhalin Island. Here are his words:

"My tears flow constantly. I was on the edge of the bottomless pit. Now I see others are standing there. How many of them are falling into it! Dear Lord....help those who do not know You yet! Lord, put their feet on Your path!"

WHAT A PLEA AND BURDEN FROM SOMEONE IN EXILE. HOW UNSELFISH THAT HE WOULD SEE OTHERS AS LOST AND DYING! IT WOULD DEFINITELY BE DIFFICULT TO BE EXILED, ISOLATED FROM ANY FORM OF CONTACT. YET BITTER ISOLATION BECOMES SWEET AS WE INVOKE THE WONDROUS PRESENCE OF OUR LOVING AND CARING FATHER. SUCH EXPERIENCES DEEPEN OUR FAITH AND MAKE US AWARE OF HIM. IN WHAT WAYS HAVE YOU FOUND ISOLATION TO BE HELPFUL TO YOUR CHRISTIAN WALK?

Verse: "Be still, and know that I am God: I will be exalted among the nations, I will be exalted in the earth." (PSALM 46:10)

Beauty for Ashes:
A Cambodian
Journey to Salvation

*I*t began four years ago when Som's wife fell critically ill. He went to consult the local faith healer, or "Kru," desperate to find a cure. The Kru told Som that he must collect pollen from the flower of the date palm tree and make a special paste from it for his wife.

Finding the tree was easy -- climbing it was more difficult. But Som was determined and made his way up the trunk. At the top, he reached for a palm branch, pulling it toward him to get to the pollen. His feet slipped and he fell to the ground, breaking his back and leaving him paralyzed from the waist down.

> **"Knowing Christ changed Som so dramatically that he has been instrumental in leading others to the Lord."**

Som changed almost overnight. He became an embittered, broken man, full of resentment towards his wife and God. Sometime later, a caring Christian stopped at his home, prayed for Som and gave him a Bible. Although Som neither believed in nor understood the God of the man who prayed for him, he opened the book and read. Two days later, Som tuned to an FEBC broadcast for the first time. Step by step, listening to the programs and reading his new Bible, Som began to grasp the meaning of the message. It soon led him to accept Christ.

Hearing the Word of the Lord over the radio and absorbing the solid teaching of FEBC broadcasters profoundly impacted his bitterness, and peace restored his broken soul.

Knowing Christ changed Som so dramatically that he has been instrumental in leading others to the Lord. In spite of his disability, the Lord uses him as an evangelist in Cambodia, as well as a leader in the church — a counselor people turn to for advise and personal ministry.

No wonder the Bible refers to the Word as being sharper than any two-edged sword. For Som and many of his countrymen, FEBC's Gospel broadcasts have cut through the chains of despair, freeing them to possess God's promised "... beauty for ashes, the oil of joy for mourning... that they may be called trees of righteousness, the planting of the Lord, that He may be glorified " (Isaiah 61:3).

IT IS SAID THAT MAN'S DISAPPOINTMENTS ARE GOD'S APPOINTMENTS. EVERYTHING THAT HAPPENS TO YOU IS FOR A PURPOSE. WHAT YOU THOUGHT WOULD BE A HOPELESS SITUATION CAN BE TURNED AROUND BY GOD FOR HIS GLORY. OUR LORD IS THE GOD OF IMPOSSIBILITIES AND HE HAS THE POWER AND THE WISDOM TO DIRECT YOUR LIFE IN THE WAY THAT IS BEST FOR YOU. ONLY TRUST HIM NOW! WHAT DISAPPOINTMENTS IN YOUR LIFE CAN YOU GIVE TO THE LORD, TRUSTING HIS PLAN FOR YOUR LIFE?

Verse: *"Why are you downcast, O my soul? Why so disturbed within me? Put your hope in God, for I will yet praise Him, my Savior and my God."* - (PSALM 42:11)

Story 11

Set Free from Satan

*F*or years I lived a meaningless and confused life despite all my efforts to make it the other way around. I lived in fear. I would often carry around with me two guns which gave me a feeling of security and superiority. My "manly" lifestyle consisted of a good smoke, a good drink and sex. And yet I was a religious man. I even became a 32nd degree Mason.

In spite of all this, the unidentifiable need of my life remained. I would ask myself, "Was I born only to eat, wear good clothes and earn a living?" Finding no satisfactory answer and with circumstances working against me and my family, I finally decided one day in 1968 to end it all. But as I pressed my gun against my temple, I thought of my innocent family. I couldn't pull the trigger.

I then turned to the invisible world of demonic powers. Fortune tellers and horoscopes were my counselors and guides. I dabbled in hypnotism, mind power, cosmic magnetism, transcendental meditation and yoga. These later led me to be a medium and a psychic healer. Exorcisms, visions, trances, astral or out of the body travels and automatic writing were routine to us at home. We could see and communicate with different spirits-- spirits of the "dead," "saints" as well as those from "other planets." We had seen graven images move and assume different facial expressions. The devil loves to trick and deceive people.

The most puzzling experience I had, however, was when our spirit guide instructed us to buy a Bible to read and to study certain portions of it. This led to my intellectual confusion but later to my spiritual enlightenment. I soon discovered discrepancies between what the spirit guide taught us and what I read in the Bible. I was so greatly confused that toward the end of 1974, I literally cried out to God, admitting my confusion, my ignorance as well as my lack of control over the spirits and over what was happening to me and my family. I then decided to renounce all my occult and psychic powers and practices and begged God to enlighten me further.

In the latter part of 1975, I accidentally tuned in my radio to a religious program called **Unshackled** aired over DZAS of the Far East Broadcasting Company. Thinking it was another religious gimmick, my first impulse was to turn it off for fear of being misled. But something told me it coincided with the truth I had learned from my continuous study of the Bible. I learned from the program that one needed to trust Jesus Christ as personal Lord and Savior. So I was encouraged daily to listen to this particular station.

The radio programs directed me and some of the members of my household to a missions office which later directed us to a church (Capital City Alliance Church in Quezon City). It was here that I was baptized and where I learned more about the Bible and where I worshipped and served God. Today, I am serving the Lord in Bacolod through Armor Ministries.

Now instead of consulting fortune tellers, spirit guides, occult books and horoscopes, I consult Christ and His word, the Bible. I have disposed of all my firearms. My life is in God's hands and my security is in Him. I no longer need yoga, transcendental meditation, hypnotism and religion to attain tranquility in life. Since I have peace with God, I also have the peace of God in my life. Praise God, I AM FREE !

- Oscar Emmanuel Cruz

WHEN SOMEONE COMES TO CHRIST, SEEKING FOR TRUTH, HE WILL NEVER BE DISAPPOINTED. JESUS CHRIST IS THE ONE WHO RELEASES THOSE WHO ARE IN BONDAGE OF SIN AND OCCULT PRACTICES. HE HAS COME TO DESTROY THE WORKS OF THE DEVIL. IT IS IN THE NAME OF JESUS CHRIST THAT WE HAVE THE VICTORY AND WE CAN CLAIM FREEDOM. ARE THERE ANY SINFUL PRACTICES IN YOUR LIFE THAT YOU NEED TO BE RELEASED FROM?

Verse: *Christ said, "So if the Son sets you free, you will be free indeed."*
- *(JOHN 8:36)*

Story 12

From the Land of the Rising Sun

*H*itoshi Ono wrote FEBC for the first time on September 6, 1994. He had been listening to the English broadcasts coming out of Manila's short-wave service. What follows is a chronicle of his spiritual journey through his correspondence with

Roger Foyle, FEBC's head of the Overseas English Audience Relations Department. Roger faithfully replied to all his letters, answering his questions and providing him with Gospel tracts and literature. Hitoshi and Roger have become good friends since. In December 1997, Hitoshi visited FEBC Manila to meet the Overseas English staff workers who were overjoyed to see him.

Hitoshi Ono - Japanese listener who got converted to Christ through the broadcasts.

6TH SEPTEMBER 1994

"This is my first letter to write to your station. I always listen as long as I can and your station always brings us lots of information about Asia, especially the Philippines. Though I am Buddhist, I am interested in Christian Science, because once I was in University here in Japan I took American literature course and its textbook included poems from Christian Science Monitor."

10TH DECEMBER 1994

"I have been thinking that all of your programmes give us knowledge about the Lord Jesus Christ with other very useful topics. Since I received your letter and programme guide, I have been thinking about the relations between the Lord and my life......

I also listen to other radio stations, but I've never written to them. This is because my favorite station is your FEBC Philippines....I feel much happy that you read my letter in your programme (Let's Hear from You).

May I ask you my questions?

Why had he need to die on the cross for human beings?
Why does Jesus forgive our sin?
How can I follow the Lord Jesus Christ?"

24ᵀᴴ JANUARY 1995

"The special programmes on this Christmas season were full of fascination to me. They all help me to understand what Christmas means."

21ˢᵀ FEBRUARY 1995

"I listened to *Good Morning from Manila* yesterday and enjoyed your programme. FEBC tells us to accept the Lord and we will be sure to go to heaven. I will follow your way to life, not Buddhism. The Lord is the Savior to human beings, isn't he?

16ᵀᴴ MAY 1995

"Thank you for sending me the booklet, 'The Lord Jesus Christ' (The Life with a Difference). I enjoyed reading again and again. Nowadays, I realize that the more I listen to FEBC, the more I comprehend about....seeking my living God. It is clear that I need Jesus to solve my personal problems. All I have to do now is accept the ways of Christ......Someday I really keep in touch with God."

1ˢᵀ AUGUST 1995

"You told me in your letter that Jesus is the way to God and if I wish to become a born again Christian, I need to be joined to Christ. Let me know the way to be joined to Christ. I quote my favorite sentence again: "If we are faithless, He remains faithful" (11Tim 2 v 13). I think human nature is imperfect, so Christ died for our sin.

13TH OCTOBER 1995

"I received two letters from your station last month. They showed me how deep is your love.....In this letter, I would like to let you know something about my personal invitation to Jesus.

It is a fact that I saw a miracle-gloomy light was flashing for a moment when I was reading Bible, praying my future to Jesus....(It was) on the first day of October about 02.00 JST (Japan Standard Time). The other day, 7th October, I visited an evangelical church in Matsuyama. The staff did prayer for me and gave me the New Testament in Japanese....At last, I could take my first step towards the Lord. So I do believe your words, 'Jesus is the way.....' I can hear His voice in person when I pray and meditate in silence. I wonder I can do (that)....I never forget the time when I had cried out, listening to your programmes."

13TH NOVEMBER 1995

"Again, Mr. Roger, I would like to tell you whatever I think of Jesus....Now I am trying the Good News Bible Course. The teaching will help me to understand how deep Jesus loves us! If I have time, I would like to attend Sunday Sermon in Matsuyama. Christmas season will come very soon. This year I will celebrate because this Christmas will be the first since I started my new life, so I am looking forward to having a party......"

17TH DECEMBER 1995

At last I will be baptized on this Christmas Day... I had started to attend worship service on Sundays, and pray for happiness in that evangelical church in Matsuyama.....I feel so happy to receive his grace.....I know it has only just begun, my fellowship with God and His Son, Jesus. I trust and believe in Him all through my life, even after death."

11TH JANUARY 1996

"Now I really enjoy my life as a Christian with my pastor and other friends who live in Matsuyama. I am proud of that church, though some of my friends felt curiously of my baptism."

25TH AUGUST 1997

"To you all at FEBC, I always bear in mind about your counsel. I know how to go forward step by step. You are my best friends if you allow me to think so. So keep up the good work to preach the Gospel to the world!"

13TH DECEMBER 1997 (EMAIL)

"I praise the Lord Jesus. I have received latest letter from Mr. Roger. And of course Maria and I will be able to visit you this time. I still cannot believe that I will go there in the Philippines and meet Mrs. Fay, Madini and also "the gang."*

MISSIOLOGISTS WOULD CONTEND THAT JAPAN IS ONE OF THE COUNTRIES IN THE WORLD THAT IS VERY DIFFICULT TO REACH WITH THE GOSPEL. LESS THAN 1% OF ITS 128 MILLION INHABITANTS ARE CHRISTIANS. THERE ARE MANY OBSTACLES FACED BY MISSIONARIES: THE DIFFICULTIES OF THE LANGUAGE AND SCRIPT, COMPLEXITIES OF THE CULTURE, DEMONIC FORCES PERVADING ANCESTOR WORSHIP IN HOMES. YET GOD IN HIS ALMIGHTY POWER IS WORKING IN JAPAN. PRAISE HIM FOR PEOPLE WHO GET SAVED THROUGH THE FAITHFUL WITNESS OF BELIEVERS AS WELL AS OTHER MEANS LIKE GOSPEL BROADCASTS. HOW CAN YOU PRAY FOR THE PEOPLE OF JAPAN TO COME TO CHRIST?

Verse: "*Devote yourself to prayer, keeping alert in it with an attitude of thanksgiving; praying at the same time for us as well, that God may open to us a door for the word, so that we may speak forth the mystery of Christ.*" (COLOSSIANS 4: 2-3)

---

* (Overseas English Staff)

Be Merciful to Me, A Sinner

*T*he old-timers living in Olongapo, Philippines, near Subic Bay, once the home of the American Seventh Fleet, will tell you that Basilio Clark, the warm Baptist pastor who plays a guitar and sings so beautifully, is a far different person from the one who terrorized the same city in his youth.

Basilio's father was an American serviceman, his mother a Filipina who met and fell in love with the handsome American. After several children were born, Basilio's father was killed in an automobile accident. Without enough food at home, Basilio began to run the streets, stealing from the sidewalk vendors and shopkeepers in the open markets of Olongapo.

"Mixing insecticide, which had been smuggled into the prison, with stolen paint thinner, the nine of them formed a circle and drank the deadly potion."

As a teenager, Basilio was the head of a gang that robbed, plundered, murdered, and pillaged at will. They were captured after a long manhunt and were sentenced to die in the electric chair. Fearing death by electrocution, Basilio and his gang of eight chose rather to die at their own hands.

Mixing insecticide, which had been smuggled into the prison, with stolen paint thinner, the nine of them formed a circle and drank the deadly potion. Of the nine, only one survived: Basilio, and he became blind.

He had failed in life and he had failed in death. While he awaited his appointment with the electric chair, Basilio began listening to the radio which Olga Robertson, a faithful prison worker, had given to the prisoners. This little radio, known as a PM (Portable Missionary) played but one station, DZAS, the voice of the Far East Broadcasting Company. Day after day as Basilio listened, God spoke to his heart until he got converted.

Gaining Basilio's confidence, Olga Robertson discipled and taught him the Word of God, and he in turn, told the other prisoners that God had forgiven him and that he repented of his sins.

When he was issued a presidential pardon, Basilio returned to Olongapo a changed man and there continued to share his faith with others.

What God did for a gangster like Basilio, He can do for you. Changed life is what the Gospel of Jesus Christ is all about. Paul was right, *"If anyone is in Christ, he is a new creation...."* (2 Corinthians 5:17)

GOD HAS A PLAN FOR EVERY PERSON'S LIFE NO MATTER HOW TOTALLY WASTED AT THE OUTSET IT SEEMS TO BE. WHEN SOMEONE COMES TO KNOW JESUS CHRIST AS HIS PERSONAL SAVIOR AND LORD, HE BRINGS NEW HOPE TO THE PERSON AND A NEW DIRECTION IN LIFE. LIFE TAKES ON A DIFFERENT MEANING. ONCE IT WAS USED FOR SINFUL PLEASURE AND SELFISH GAIN, NOW IT IS USED FOR SERVING GOD AND BRINGING OTHERS TO HIS KINGDOM. WHAT NEW PURPOSES AND DIRECTIONS IN YOUR LIFE HAVE BEEN BROUGHT ABOUT AS A RESULT OF YOUR COMING TO JESUS CHRIST?

Verse: *"for it is God who works in you to will and to act according to His good purpose."* (PHILIPPIANS 2:13)

Hope for a Cancer Patient in China

*M*r. Tan (not his real name) was a card-bearing member of the Communist Party, high in the hierarchy as a regional party chairman. Mrs. Tan was the manager of one of the radio stations in the city. The family enjoyed a comfortable life befitting high ranking members of the Party.

But there was a dark cloud hovering over their sunny world, a source of great pain in their lives. Their daughter, My Lian, was suffering from incurable bone cancer.

"There was nothing in their communist faith that could bring them comfort during this time of darkness."

My Lian had been bedridden since she contracted the disease. Weak and in pain, she had lost hope. Her parents were resigned to the fact that as days go by, this lovely daughter would simply waste away; one day she would finally be lost from them forever. There was nothing in their communist faith that could bring them comfort during this time of darkness.

My Lian herself was desperate. She wished she was dead. One day, in her loneliness, she sought the companionship of her radio. As she fiddled with the dial, she happened to tune in to the Mandarin broadcasts of FEBC coming from Iba, Zambales, Philippines.

The man at the other end talked about hope amidst hopeless situations, forgiveness and healing. He talked about Jesus Christ who was powerful and merciful. For My Lian, these were strange but comforting words. As the broadcaster ended his program with a prayer, My Lian prayed with him...claiming for herself the deliverance that Jesus Christ was giving to anyone who would call upon Him.

As she prayed, she received not only cleansing from sin, but also a miraculous healing of her cancer! Having been bedridden for a long time, she eagerly tested her feet and started to walk. Then she went down to the ground floor of their home...where she found her dumbfounded parents staring at her...afraid that she might be an apparition of their daughter, now dead.

Excitedly she shared with them what God had done to her through the power of the Lord Jesus Christ. They, too, started listening to the broadcasts. They began to learn about Jesus Christ — His life, His works, His words. Today the Tan family worships God together.

LONELINESS IS SAID TO BE ONE MAJOR CAUSE OF SUICIDE. YOU MAY FEEL LIKE YOU HAVE NO ONE TO TURN TO AND THAT YOU ARE AT THE END OF YOUR ROPE. HOW WILL YOU SURVIVE WHEN YOUR VERY REASON FOR EXISTENCE IS BEING CHALLENGED? THE SECRET IS IN LIVING IN THE SHADOW OF OUR OMNIPRESENT GOD WHO HAS PROMISED NEVER TO ABANDON US. IN WHAT WAYS CAN GOD EASE THE LONELINESS IN YOUR LIFE?

Verse: *"God has said, 'Never will I leave you; never will I forsake you."*
(HEBREWS 13:5)

Story 15

A Witch Doctor No More

"*Hummmmmm...balaya.....*" the wizard started folding his hands across his chest in prayer to his gods. "*Hmmmmmmmmm... balaya*" his chants echo throughout the small hut as his young patient squirms with pain. Outside his hut several other patients form queues, waiting for their turn. In this small village of Taung-ka-lon in Myanmar, Saw Aung has earned quite a reputation. He was known as the wizard.

In his younger days, Saw Aung was part of the patriotic partisans who fought the British side by side with the Japanese during the Second World War. Then again he fought the Japanese alongside the British army. But not long after Myanmar's independence in 1948, this time battling against insurgents, Saw Aung sustained a serious injury that paralyzed him from his waist down. The Myanmar government gave him an honorable discharge with full pension and assigned a permanent nurse to care for him. Later, he married this nurse and after two years a daughter was born to them.

During this time, a dark realization came to Saw Aung — he would never be able to walk again. In his desperation, he resorted to spiritism, occult and witchcraft. These practices became his main source of livelihood. He became a well-known witch doctor and people referred to him as the wizard who cures sickness by reciting charms to his gods. In return for his services, the people offered him money, food and other material things.

The Lord however had a better plan for his life. Three years ago, he came to hear of the love, peace and forgiveness that can only be found in Jesus Christ through Christian radio.

At once he became interested in the program and he started to hunger for the teachings of Jesus. He accepted Jesus in his life without anybody around to help him.

Listeners in Myanmar similar to those in the Witch Doctor's village.

Later, Saw Aung wrote to FEBC. His first letter was followed by more letters as the Myanmar program producers nurtured him through the broadcasts and correspondence. Through counseling and follow-up, he realized the need to publicly confess his faith through baptism. Eventually, he requested a pastor from a nearby church to baptize him.

Today, Saw Aung walks through life with Jesus in his heart. The Lord turned his life and led him out of his dark past... The lips he once used to utter chants and charms are now lips that declare praise and worship to our Lord.

★ SINCE THE 70'S, FEBC HAS BEEN BROADCASTING THE GOSPEL TO MYANMAR, NOW IN 17 LANGUAGES AND DIALECTS. ASIDE FROM BEING KNOWN AS THE WORLD'S MAJOR EXPORTER OF OPIUM, THE COUNTRY HAS ALSO BEEN A SPIRITUAL FORTRESS OF BUDDHISM. MANY PEOPLE, PARTICULARLY IN TRIBAL AREAS, RESORT TO WITCHCRAFT AND SPIRITISM. ONLY GOD CAN BREAK THESE STRONGHOLDS AND AS WE BELIEVE HIS PROMISES TOGETHER, WE CAN EXPECT THAT MORE PEOPLE WILL COME TO HEAR THE GOOD NEWS OF SALVATION. HAVE YOU DEVELOPED THAT PRAYERFUL CONCERN FOR THE LOST IN OTHER LANDS?

Verse: *"Everyone who calls on the name of the Lord will be saved."*
- (ROMANS 10:13)

Story 16

Not by Works of Righteousness

S ince I was a youth, I was devoted to the religion of my forefathers. I was fervent in my attendance of church activities such as studying the catechism, praying the rosary, praying for the souls of the dead and confessing to the priest. I was also one of those who would go on my knees from the door up to the altar of the church in Quiapo with the belief that God would hear me if I did all these things. Devoted to the Virgin Mary, I thought that she was the sole mediator between God and man, the only way to the Father and the only one who could give me eternal life.

"Many trials in my life have come and gone and through all these Christ has been my Strength."

In spite of all these, I was confused and had many questions in my mind as I journeyed on in this life. Gradually these questions began to find answers when I married a Christian man who took me to fellowships and Bible studies. I had a fervent desire to find out the truth, whether I was embracing the right faith. At first I did not listen to the believers who were sharing God's Word with me but instead I turned my back on them and continued in my religious activities.

As life went on, I had seven children and in order to pass the time away at home, I would turn on the radio. On one of these days at 6 o'clock in the morning, I happened to tune in to a program called *Hardin ng*

Panalangin. The message that morning was on the true Savior, the Lord Jesus Christ. The pastor said that He was the only way to life – this Christ, whom I only remember on Christmas and Easter. From then on I thirsted for the Word of God as I always read it and listened to the radio messages. It was in 1980 that I received Jesus Christ as my personal Lord and Savior. I took part then in Bible studies and the Holy Spirit began to work in my life.

Many trials in my life have come and gone and through all these Christ has been my Strength. I have left my old ways that have not been pleasing to the Lord. I realized that the works I did since I was a youth were filthy rags in the sight of the Lord. The Lord has now been using me in church to serve Him. I am always ready to testify on what the Lord has done to save me from my wrong and misguided beliefs and bring me to true faith in Him. Now I can face any trial knowing that my precious Savior goes with me wherever I go.

-- Mrs. Julieta Ocampo

THE REALIZATION THAT ONE'S OWN GOOD WORKS CANNOT SAVE OR BRING US TO HEAVEN IS THE FIRST STEP NEARER THE KINGDOM. NOT UNTIL WE ACKNOWLEDGE THAT WE CANNOT SAVE OURSELVES ON OUR OWN CAN WE TRULY BE SAVED AS WE TRUST IN THE FINISHED WORK OF CHRIST ON THE CROSS. IT IS BY GOD'S WONDERFUL MERCY AND GRACE THAT HE DRAWS US TO HIM IF WE COME JUST AS WE ARE. IN WHAT WAYS ARE YOU TRUSTING IN YOUR OWN GOOD WORKS AND RELIGIOSITY TO BRING YOU TO HEAVEN?

Verse: *"For it is by grace you have been saved through faith- and this not from yourselves, it is the gift of God; not by works, that no one can boast."* (EPHESIANS 2:8-9)

Story 17

The Rewards of Fervent Prayer

*L*et's go to Bocos, Banaue, Ifugao -- way up in the northern part of the Philippines. Our story unfolds in the home of Albert Dagoh who was born again in December of 1987.

When he just received the Lord as his Savior, he was spiritually "high" and shared his new found faith with his father as soon as he arrived at home. Albert's father was a high priest in their animistic religion. Those who grow up in animistic faiths worship and appease spirits that live in animals, trees, stones and other inanimate objects.

Albert was discouraged and felt rejected because his father looked at him like he was still a young child. He even reasoned out that Albert had no experience in life. His father said he did not need the Gospel.

"His father said he did not need the Gospel."

But Albert did not give up. He asked for the Lord's help. The following morning at 10:30 a.m. he found his transistor radio and it so happened that it was tuned to FEBC's radio broadcasts from Manila. He heard a drama called *Tanikalang Lagot* where the story was about a son and his alcoholic father. At the end of that drama, the son was so frustrated but he just constantly prayed to God to change his drunkard father. Able to identify himself with the son in the drama, Albert was encouraged to pray fervently for his animist father. He committed the situation to the Lord despite his frustrations over his father who violently disturbed their home to the point of causing his sisters to rebel.

In praying that his father be changed, the Lord brought about a situation that caused his father to make a "U" turn.

In June 1991, Albert's father met a vehicular accident where he fractured his left leg. While in the hospital, Albert took the time to witness to his father. Before his discharge God confirmed to Albert that his father would leave his old traditional animistic life.

Upon his father's return home, he invited all their relatives. Together with his Christian friends, Albert shared God's Word. That ushered in a new start for his family for on that day Albert's father accepted Jesus Christ as his Savior.

IT IS WONDERFUL TO KNOW THAT WHENEVER AND WHEREVER GOD'S WORD IS PREACHED IT DOES NOT RETURN VOID. HIS WORD IS LIKE SEED WHICH IS SOWN IN THE HEART OF A PERSON AND WHEN THE SOIL OF THE HEART IS CULTIVATED THROUGH PRAYER AND LIFE'S CIRCUMSTANCES, THAT SEED WILL GROW AND BRING FORTH FRUIT. YOU CAN ALWAYS COUNT ON THE WORD OF GOD TO ACCOMPLISH HIS WILL. HOW ARE YOU SOWING THE SEED OF THE WORD IN THE HEARTS OF OTHERS, PARTICULARLY YOUR FAMILY?

Verse: *"So is My Word that goes out from My mouth: it will not return to Me empty, but will accomplish what I desire, and achieve the purpose for which I sent it."* (ISAIAH 55:11)

Vietnamese Village Miracle

*I*n 1996, Toan Tran Humprey visited her homeland Vietnam after 27 years. It was in this trip that she saw the Lord's hand working in the lives of Christians. This story is an excerpt from her report... a modern day story of Peter, the apostle of hope... enduring pain, persecution and prison... to go on believing, hoping and obeying Christ.

July 17, 1996

"On June 23, 1996 I attended a church at Cam Ranh Bay. The pastor there is not allowed to preach, because he said something that offended the government. Elders and laymen run the church. There were less than 100 people attending the service. More than half of them are from tribes who come on foot or on bicycles with their children on their back. Some even had to travel 10 miles to hear God's Word.

"That village was known for people being alcoholic and extremely superstitious. They sacrificed animals for worship. The government had tried to change their way of life but failed."

During Sunday School, I stood outside and had a chat with one of their members. She told me that in the 17 years that the church was closed, she and her family were fed and nurtured spiritually by listening to FEBC broadcasts. She also told me that there are many people who came to know the Lord through listening to FEBC, especially tribal people.

> *"The elders have been arrested, jailed and beaten up many times but with a smile, they told me that they will go on until the day the Lord calls them home."*

Later I met with two of the church elders. They told me of the same story of how many tribal people came to know Christ through the broadcasts. They particularly told me of the story of one village, where 107 people were converted to Christ. The government sent *"Pho Chu Tich Cong An"* (Police Chief Assistant) to investigate and to make life difficult for them so they will stop listening to FEBC and believing in God. But this police listened to FEBC and became a Christian himself. When authorities discovered this, he was removed from the village and from his duty. No one knows where he is right now.

That village was known for people being alcoholic and extremely superstitious. They sacrificed animals for worship. The government had tried to change their way of life but failed. Since they came to know the Lord, they have been set free from all their addictions and bondage to evil. But instead of rejoicing with the villagers, the government sent police authorities to punish them.

These people had to flee deeper into the mountains. The two elders with whom I spoke have been coming to visit, to pray and to have Bible Study with them. The elders have been arrested, jailed and beaten up many times but with a smile, they told me that they will go on until the day the Lord calls them home.

How beautiful are the feet of those who bring good news, this verse came to my mind as I looked at the elders. My heart is full of gratitude for these men. I asked them what their most crucial need was, and they said Bibles and radios. I was able to give them some money for this purpose, and some to use as they see fit when they visit the tribe. They broke down in tears and told me that they have been visiting the sick yet they have no money to buy anything for these people.

With this trip, I learned of the effect of Christian radio in people's lives. I remember the pastors who will eventually die. With no Bible schools, who will carry on the work? But I am reminded of God, the Creator of all things — it is His work to bring people to the saving knowledge of His Son. I know that He has used FEBC to do just that and also nurture believers in their walk with Him. To God be the glory..."

No other god on earth can perform awesome and wondrous miracles that the God of the Bible has manifested. To this day, He still displays His grace and power through the lives of countless people that have been changed by the Gospel message. How can we not help but praise Him for His awesome works? Are you giving thanks to God for His salvation in every tribe and nation?

Verse: *"After this I looked and there before me was a great multitude, that no one could count, from every nation, tribe, people and language, standing before the throne and in front of the Lamb..."* (REVELATION 7:9)

The Crisis in Batia

*B*atia had been a peaceful community in Bulacan before Communist aggression forced it to make a decision. The folk were pressured to either bear arms against the government or turn their farming settlement into a food supply center for the *Huks* (local version of Communist rebels at that time). They chose to do the latter.

Batia Baptist Church in the 1980's.

Little did they know that such decision would cost some of them their lives. One night in the early 50's, government trucks towing light artillery stopped beside a road and were waiting behind the bamboo clumps, 500 yards away. As usual that evening, Huks swarmed in from the countryside to carry food supplies to their bases in the foothills. Without warning, the government canon belched forth its deadly shells and spewed shrapnel in the center of the village. Screams of pain were heard from the passersby. Homes got burned down and twelve people died.

One of the men of Batia had been listening to the radio, weeks before. Without fail he listened and wondered whether he was listening to some new form of propaganda. Communism had made numerous promises but this voice on the radio spoke of personal joy and security. Feliciano listened to FEBC night after night until he was faced with a decision to accept Christ as his Savior.

When he made that commitment what a difference it brought in his life! Folks at Batia noticed him and asked one another what had happened. Feliciano told his friends about the messages he had been hearing on the radio and so nightly, the villagers began to tune in. It became not only a popular means of diversion but it did something more to the hearts of the listeners. Gradually they too changed because of the Gospel message and became a strong influence on the villagers.

Four months after that dreadful night, six men from Batia arrived at the FEBC Compound (known as Christian Radio City Manila) in Valenzuela. Bringing their mats and food, these young Christians requested that they be trained in soul-winning, and after three weeks of intensive study at FEBC, they returned to their town fired with witnessing zeal.

Later they invited radio evangelist Max Atienza to visit their place. At first Max was hesitant because he thought that it might endanger his life but when he arrived at Batia, the villagers asked him if FEBC was a Communist front. Max was shocked to find out that they thought such but they later told him that they had lost their confidence in Communism because of their broken promises. They also wanted to find out in person if the messages they were hearing from the radio were true.

Max therefore took the opportunity to explain the way of salvation. He found out that 31 of the villagers had been saved through the witness of the six men who spent the short time at FEBC and many were faithfully listening to the radio each evening. Because of the interest in spiritual things and the building of a small chapel which later became known as Batia Baptist Church, the spirit of the Huks had been broken in that area. Like uncontrollable fire, the Gospel message spread through the homes of Batia and the surrounding countryside. But this is not the end of the Batia story...

The Undersecretary of National Defense at that time, heard of what happened to Batia from the then FEBC Director, Richard Bronson. Bronson tried to get him to visit the place and accompanied him to Batia. When the Undersecretary arrived there, he talked with the villagers himself and found out that from the conversion of this one man, Feliciano Cristobal, the Gospel message spread until two years later, thirteen churches had started in barrios nearby. The Undersecretary was so overwhelmed by what he witnessed that he couldn't keep this to himself as he saw the changes in the town itself and in the people's lives.

That evening, he called President Magsaysay (Philippine President at the time) and told him what he saw. Late that night, without bodyguards, the President had his chauffeur drive him to the barrio of Batia to see for himself what happened. The President could hardly believe his eyes. He saw first hand what had happened and talked with the many villagers concerning their belief. He told the Undersecretary, "This thing is unbelievable. What has happened here is what we want to happen in other places. We must tell this story and give this message to our people. In fact, we must share this with the peoples of Asia. This will change the very course of the Communists. We must do everything we can help to get this story to our people and to the nation around us. Call the manager of DZAS right away and tell him we want to do everything we can to help get this story out".

Although President Magsaysay's vision died with him in the plane crash that took his life, the vision of Batia still lives on. Batia Baptist Church became the first church on record that was born as a direct result of FEBC broadcasts. It has grown and been instrumental in the birth of other local churches. And what happened to Feliciano Cristobal? He became a dedicated worker in FEBC for twenty years, serving the Lord as foreman of antenna maintenance in the transmitter site of Bocaue, Bulacan.

THE WITNESS OF ONE PERSON, TOTALLY YIELDED TO THE WORK OF GOD CAN BRING FORTH A HARVEST OF SPIRITUAL FRUIT. AS LONG AS OUR LIVES ARE YIELDED AND WE ARE READY TO BE USED FOR HIS GLORY, HIS LIGHT WILL CONTINUE TO SHINE TO TRANSFORM PLACES OF DARKNESS TO BEACONS OF LIGHT. IN WHAT WAYS CAN YOU IMPACT YOUR NEIGHBORHOOD OR COMMUNITY FOR CHRIST?

Verse: *"Let your light shine before men, that they may see your good deeds and praise your Father in heaven."* -- (MATTHEW 5:16)

Nothing
is Impossible

*S*ean Gabriel Baylon was born August 18, 1997. But he was born prematurely. Imagine the anxiety his parents Clyde and Melissa had when they learned that his lungs were not fully developed. Upon birth, their baby had to be placed in an incubator with a ventilator hose for his lungs to help him breathe normally.

The doctor at a hospital in Manila gave Sean a 50% chance to get over this abnormal condition, discouraging his parents from hoping for an improvement. Aside from this were the risks of possible infections and further complications that would result from being put in a ventilator for some time.

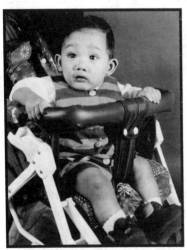

Baby Sean Gabriel Baylon .

Sean's parents were informed ahead of time that the cost of the baby's treatment could amount to between P250,000 and P500,000. Because of this humongous expense, the doctor had a heart-to-heart talk with Sean's Dad. He told him that it would be up to them to decide whether to keep the ventilator plugged throughout the required duration and bear the total cost against an uncertain outcome or just allow nature to take its course and pull out the plug when they could no longer shoulder the cost.

Sean's Dad tells it in his own words: "I knew God wanted Sean to live, for had He not, He would not have put life in our baby's body at birth. So I decided on the ventilator machine for Sean, no matter the cost, as my own part in giving him a slim chance to live with the full knowledge that only God can give and take the same life as He wills."

He and his wife surrendered everything to the Lord, praying each day for their baby's progress. And God, in His faithfulness and mercy began the healing process in Sean's body.

One night, as the couple tuned in to the evening **Heartline** program, it so happened that the topic for the week was "Mercy Killing and Abortion". The program caught their attention and immediately they called FEBC to share about their baby. Gratitude and peace reigned in their hearts when at the end of the program, Carmen Vargas, the counselor, prayed for baby Sean's healing. Not only that, he was prayed for in *Hardin Ng Panalangin* and other radio programs.

God intervened in the situation and answered their prayers in His perfect time. Instead of the prescribed two weeks on the ventilator, the baby made it in just two days. His three-week stay in the incubator was also shortened and the huge medical bill in the range of P250,000 to P500,000 was settled at P89,000. In less than a month, Sean went home to the waiting arms of his mother, fully well and healthy. The couple learned that, indeed, nothing is impossible with God.

YOU MAY BE ASKING WHY YOU ARE GOING THROUGH A CERTAIN TRIAL OR DIFFICULTY IN LIFE. YOU KEEP PRAYING ABOUT IT BUT IT SEEMS THAT THE TRIAL WON'T GO AWAY; THE PROBLEM KEEPS GETTING BIGGER. LIFE'S TRIALS DO SERVE A PURPOSE FOR WITHOUT THEM OUR FAITH WOULD NOT GROW, WE WOULD NOT COME TO KNOW GOD IN A DEEPER WAY. WE WOULD NOT FIND OUT THAT HE IS THE GOD WHO CAN WORK THROUGH IMPOSSIBLE SITUATIONS. IN WHAT WAYS HAS YOUR FAITH BEEN TESTED IN THE PAST?

Verse: *"For nothing is impossible with God"* (LUKE 1:37)

Story 21

In the Face of Persecution

*M*yanmar, formerly known as Burma, is the largest country in the Southeast Asian Peninsula with a population of over 45 million. The term Myanmar embraces 135 ethnic groups; speaking over a hundred different languages and dialects.

The ancient people of Myanmar were the prime movers of Therawada Buddhism. Majority of its people are worshippers of Buddha. In the cities, elaborately decorated pagodas or temples of worship for Buddha can be seen everywhere. One place in Myanmar, the City of Bagan, is known as the city of four million pagodas. These temples house the remains of Buddha and his followers, his sacred writings, images, statues and utensils. These are where Buddhists offer their gifts and pay homage to their god.

In provinces and villages, a pagoda that houses images of Buddha stands in the center of each village. It is in these villages where people are so akin to each other, that it becomes difficult to live as a believer of Jesus Christ.

Here is a letter sent by a young student which clearly pictures the difficulty and persecution their family had experienced in the hands of the monks and the villagers:

Listeners in Myanmar tuned to broadcasts coming from Manila.

" Dear Aunty, (their customary way of addressing an elder woman)

I hope you will be kind enough to reply to my letter.   I thank and praise the Lord that by His help, I was able to answer all the questions at our school final term examination. I believe I will pass the exam.

My father, who's from the Kadu tribe, is a very strong Buddhist. My mother is from the Kachin Tribe and a Christian. My father recently accepted Christ through your FEBC program and the chief monk from our village got very angry with him and us. To show his displeasure, he threw stones at our house which made all the villagers and our neighbors to scorn and shun us. They openly showed their hatred and refused to speak to us."

Freedom of religion is practiced in Myanmar today. But because of traditionalism, many Christians are facing persecution from the largely Buddhist population.   "What could the Christian's response be?" you may ask. Here's the rest of the letter:

" But recently they have changed and come to understand God's love and about Jesus Christ. Because when we were facing all those oppositions and hatred, our family could only get together and pray. The chief monk became curious and started listening to FEBC. He found he could not stay without listening to the message of love. After sometime he changed his attitude toward us and is friendly with us again. Praise the Lord! Please pray that the chief monk and the villagers will all come to believe in Christ."

Our brethren in closed countries cannot do anything but pray when faced with severe persecution...Pray for them and for their aggressors.

JESUS TOLD US TO TURN THE OTHER CHEEK WHEN WE ARE BEING WRONGED. HOW WE NEED HIS GRACE TO HELP US DO SO AND LOVE THOSE WHO ARE PERSECUTING US. THE MYSTERY IS THAT IN THIS LOVE WHICH COMES ONLY AS A RESULT OF ABIDING IN THE HOLY SPIRIT, PEOPLE ARE DRAWN TO CHRIST AND ALL THE MORE HE IS GLORIFIED IN OUR LIVES. IN WHAT WAYS ARE YOU RESPONDING IN LOVE TO THOSE WHO HAVE MISTREATED YOU?

Verse: *"Do not be overcome by evil, but overcome evil with good."*
- (ROMANS 12:21)

Journey of an Ex-Communist

*W*e shall call him Mr. Wu, but that is not his real name. He was born to Christian parents in Mainland China. Already in his teen years when the Communists seized power in China, young Mr. Wu was easily swayed by the blandishments of the party cadres in his province. He renounced both family ties and the faith of his parents to join the Communist party.

Pursuing a career on electronic engineering, Mr. Wu quickly rose to professorship in the college of engineering at Peking University. During his spare time he repaired radios for personal friends. One elderly man requested his assistance in repairing a family radio that was regularly used to listen to Voice of Friendship (FEBC) from the Philippines.

"He renounced both family ties and the faith of his parents to join the Communist party."

During the chaotic cultural revolution, the university where he was teaching was rocked with hostility between rival factions within the faculty and student body. The faction supported by Mr. Wu lost out in the power struggle, and he was forced out of his teaching position because of his "incorrect" views.

Disillusioned and embittered, he returned to his home province shortly before the Christmas season. Tuning to

> *"A few months after his arrival in Hong Kong, he came to Manila and paid our Chinese program staff a visit. Mr. Wu expressed his personal gratitude for the service to China rendered by FEBC. "*

his radio one night, he came across a Chinese Christmas carol being broadcast from FEBC Manila.

"Joy to the world, the Lord is come; Let earth receive her King!"

Mr. Wu was strangely warmed by these words. Joy? He had seen little of that in the party he had served so well, the party which had so recently trampled him under foot. Joy— simple human joy— was lacking in the system and its devotees upon whom he had looked as the authors of utopia. Could there, then, be any real joy in this dark gray world of the cast-iron regime?

The winsome appeal of the song would not leave him. Joy WAS to be found in the recognition of the King, a King who had already come! He became a regular listener of the FEBC Chinese broadcasts. Through these programs and the faithful witness of a friend, Mr. Wu came to know the King of kings and Lord of lords personally. And with the King came Joy!

After applying for an exit visa, he waited ten long years before being permitted to leave Mainland China, to begin life anew with relatives in Hong Kong. A few months after his arrival in Hong Kong, he came to Manila and paid our Chinese program staff a visit. Mr. Wu expressed his personal gratitude for the service to China rendered by FEBC. He went on to testify that many people in China are regular listeners of FEBC.

His final comment concerned the present-day youth of China. More and more, young people are feeling disillusioned and cheated. The party has promised much, but delivered little. In their hearts, the youth of China know full well that evil works will not bring forth peace and prosperity.

Ex-communist Wu believes the youth of China are seeking the truth, aware that it will never be found in materialism, or in mass violence. Almost every family in China has a radio, the medium that can lead them to the same Truth he met that Christmas so long ago in the strains of a familiar carol.

SOCIETY IS CHANGING VERY RAPIDLY. IN THE MIDST OF THESE CHANGES, WE MAY FEEL INSECURE, HOPELESS AND ROBBED OF OUR JOY. WE REALIZE THAT THE VERY FOUNDATION OF SOCIETY IS CRUMBLING. LET US REMEMBER TO PIN OUR HOPES IN OUR UNCHANGING GOD AND DO OUR PART IN TELLING OTHERS ABOUT HIM, THE ROCK OF OUR FOUNDATION. HOW CAN YOU HELP THE YOUTH AROUND YOU TO FIND JOY AND HOPE?

Verse: *"Jesus Christ is the same yesterday and today and forever".*
- (HEBREWS 13:8)

Story 23

Let Every Tribe and Nation

$\mathcal{E}$vangelist Paul Mortiz, together with his family of six, were excited to meet for the first time the listeners to his radio program *Bukas na Aklat*. They were no ordinary listeners; rather they were from the Dumagat tribe in the jungles of the Sierra Madre Mountains.

The Dumagats belong to the early aborigines in the Philippines. They were compelled to live in the Sierra Madre Mountains in Dibut, Quezon because lowlanders began farming in their tribal territory. Simple folk, they are dark in complexion with curly hair. Two of their assets are that they sing beautifully and have such child-like faith.

The Dumagats are spirit worshippers. Missionaries from New Tribes Mission were among the first to labor

Paul Mortiz with Dumagat believers during his visit in the 70's.

> *"Pastor Mortiz learned that the Dumagat believers had the custom of meeting for Bible study around the radio each night and discussing what they had been learning."*

among them. Their hearts proved to be fertile ground for the Gospel as souls one by one got saved.

When the Dumagats heard that their radio Bible teacher was visiting them, they were equally excited -- they longed to see the face of the voice they had been listening to. They immediately got to work building a six-room house made of bamboo and palm leaves.

Paul and Jo Mortiz arrived in Quezon that summer of 1971 with their grade-school children thrilled to meet a delegation of 200 Dumagats from five different areas ready to listen to their Bible teacher and learn at the "Bible conference". Some had traveled for three days on foot, by bus and by *banca* (canoe) to attend the conference.

Pastor Mortiz learned that the Dumagat believers had the custom of meeting for Bible study around the radio each night and discussing what they had been learning. What transpired at the conference was a blessed time of inspiration and learning from the Word of God. There was no conference "agenda " but there were three sessions daily, some lasting as long as three hours. During the last meeting, the Lord's Supper was commemorated with coconut water used as wine.

Before returning to Manila, the Mortizes visited another mission station at San Lota, which is part of the Sierra Madre mountain range. They were assisted by a missionary couple, the Quitos. When the Dumagats in this area heard they were coming, the believers requested a meeting the same evening of the Mortizes' arrival. Another meeting was held the next morning before they took their flight back to Manila. It was a blessing for Pastor Mortiz to see how hungry these people were for the Word of God.

Mrs. Mortiz recently shared that her son-in-law who is head of International Needs ministry visited the Dumagats in one of their mission trips last 1997. He reported that he met believers who grew spiritually as a result of FEBC's broadcasts and he met some who still remember their Bible teacher who visited them and the impact the radio had in their lives as a tribe way up in the Sierra Madre mountains.

GOD, OUR GREAT AND LOVING CREATOR, IS NOT CONFINED TO REACH OUT AND WORK IN ONLY ONE PEOPLE WITH ONE COLOR OF SKIN. HE IS COLOR BLIND; HE OFFERS HIS GRACE AND SALVATION TO WHOEVER COMES TO HIM. AND IN HEAVEN, WHEN WE SHALL ALL COME TOGETHER, WE WILL EXPERIENCE THE WIDENESS OF HIS MERCY AND LOVE AS WE COME FACE TO FACE WITH THE RED AND YELLOW, BLACK AND WHITE THAT ARE ALL PRECIOUS IN HIS SIGHT. THAT WILL BE GLORY! DO YOU HAVE ANY BARRIERS TOWARDS PEOPLE WHO HAVE A DIFFERENT SKIN COLOR THAN YOURS?

Verse: *"For God so loved the world that He gave his one and only Son, that whoever believes on Him shall not perish but have eternal life"*
(JOHN 3:16)

Story 24 Looking for Love

I lived as a homosexual for more than 15 years. Everything was provided for me— education, travel, a car at an early age. Yet I became very active in homosexuality at the tender age of 13. And as I went through grade school, high school and college, I had a string of female friendships and had sexual relationships with them.

When I was in second year college one of the friends I had was someone whom I loved very much. We planned to live together after college. But she died of multiple sclerosis at the age of 22. I began to rebel against God. I tried drugs and alcohol. I got into numerous cults and sects trying to find meaning in life.

I met another woman who was my last lesbian relationship. During the latter part of our relationship, we looked for an apartment where we could live together as "man and wife." That was my concept of a love relationship.

In 1985, I ended up undergoing psychiatric treatment at St. Luke's Medical Center. For two months I was under a woman psychiatrist's care. She told me, "You know, Alice, I have been counseling many homosexuals. They seem to be happy. So I tell them, 'It's all right. You can go on with the relationship.' But you're depressed. I suggest you go to another country and find a new life." I could not accept her advice. Feeling more depressed than ever, I wanted freedom from homosexuality.

I remember one time while I was staying in my girlfriend's room, I took a pen and started writing on my face, my arms and on my legs the words "I hate God, I hate myself." Then I would take acetone to erase the ink off my body and repeat the process all over again.

" I met another woman who was my last lesbian relationship. During the latter part of our relationship, we looked for an apartment where we could live together as 'man and wife.' "

One day I met a woman whom I had not seen for seven years. I hugged her tight and asked her, "Tita Norma, what are you doing out here? You look much younger than before." She answered, "I'm born again." I tried to hold back because I was thinking this might be another cult.

I love to listen to light classical music. So, every now and then, I tuned in to DZFE-FM but every time I heard Gospel music, I turned it off. I couldn't stand it.

On March 29, 1987 I turned on my radio once more. But my heart was already fertile ground because I was so desperate. I didn't want to die a homosexual. When I tuned in to DZFE I heard light classical music. A minute later, I heard somebody preach the Word of God and it was meant for me.

It was very simple— a five minute Biblical commentary by Butch Conde. He said, "If you would like to come to the Lord now and you are repentant, come to Him with tears. Repent, for the kingdom of God is at hand." At that moment, alone in my room, I surrendered my life to Jesus Christ.

Soon after this, another miracle happened. One time I went out with my aunt and I told her, "Tita, I was listening to DZFE a few nights ago and I heard this man. His name is Butch Conde." And she said, "Oh, my goodness. He is our pastor."

So I told her, "Can you please bring me there, wherever that is? I just want to see him."

I soon became a member of the Bread of Life Christian Fellowship. God has opened many doors in the area of ministry to homosexuals. My desire is to bring this ministry to many churches, to form support groups in the future. Many cannot come out of their closets because they're scared.

I thank God that because of FEBC, I was brought to a church that loves Him and lifts up His Word.

-Alice Villareal

ONE OF MAN'S GREATEST NEEDS IS THE NEED TO BE LOVED AND ACCEPTED. THERE IS ONE PERSON WHO LOVES AND ACCEPTS US UNCONDITIONALLY AND THAT IS JESUS CHRIST. HE LOVES US NOT BECAUSE OF WHO WE ARE OR WHAT WE HAVE DONE BUT IN SPITE OF WHO WE ARE AND WHAT WE HAVE DONE. SUCH THOUGHT IS LIBERATING! HAVE YOU ACCEPTED THE LORD'S UNCONDITIONAL LOVE?

Verse: "But God demonstrates His own love for us in this; while we were still sinners, Christ died for us." (ROMANS 5:8)

Story 25

God's Grace Abounding

*L*ife is hard in Myanmar. Many people are driven to engaging in illegal business just to survive. One of them is Chit Ni.

Chit Ni operated a lucrative black-market business along the Thai border. For him, money was the center of existence. Business provided him with all the money that he wanted and he was very happy.

> " He was so touched by the life of Jesus and His selfless sacrifice to save sinners like himself that he quickly accepted Him as his Savior and Lord."

Trouble came one day when the Thai police began cracking down on Burmese people doing illegal trade along the border. Chit Ni together with other Burmese nationals engaged in the same illegal trade were caught and put in prison. The Thai court sentenced Chit Ni to death for his crimes. It felt like the end of the world for him. He lost his business, his money and he was even about to lose his own life. But all was not lost.

While incarcerated in a Thai jail awaiting execution, a Thai Christian ministry held a Christmas party for the prisoners and shared the saving message of Jesus Christ. This was the first time Chit Ni heard about the Savior. He was so touched by the life of Jesus and His selfless sacrifice

> *" The Lord touched the heart of the judge and his death sentence was unexpectedly commuted to life imprisonment."*

to save sinners like himself that he quickly accepted Him as his Savior and Lord. With Jesus Christ, Chit Ni found a new lease on life.

Another inmate, an imprisoned drug dealer who owned a radio, elected to share the cell with him. One day while fiddling with his cellmate's radio, Chit Ni tuned in to the FEBC Burmese broadcast by accident. What a moment of great joy this was! Finally, the nourishment he wanted was within reach!

He immediately contacted FEBC Philippines requesting materials. A Burmese Bible and other Christian literature were immediately sent to him. These together with the regular radio broadcasts became his source of nurture and discipleship for many years.

During this time, his pending appeal with the Thai court was heard. The Lord touched the heart of the judge and his death sentence was unexpectedly commuted to life imprisonment.

There was now no stopping him from actively sharing his faith with other inmates. Fifteen people including the drug dealer received the Lord as Savior because of his efforts. Soon after, he was leading this group of new believers in Bible study. Throughout this time, he continued corresponding with Yankee Tun of FEBC Philippines.

In 1995, after serving 10 years of his sentence, he was among the prisoners pardoned by the Thai king as a special concession on the celebration of his birthday. Chit Ni's cup was now really overflowing! He was not only free but now had the ability to serve his Lord out of prison.

Chit Ni later returned to Burma after his release, joined a church and became one of its most active members.

Today, Chit Ni's desire to grow more and more like his Savior remains unquenched. He continues to be used by God in making a difference for Jesus Christ in Myanmar. Moreover, the prison ministry he started continues through the efforts of his cellmate, the reformed drug dealer, who leads the ever-growing group of believers in that Thai jail.

IMAGINE WHAT JOY WILL BE YOURS IF AFTER TEN YEARS IN JAIL, YOU WOULD BE SET FREE -- RELEASED TO JOIN THE WORLD AS A FREE PERSON AGAIN. YET GREATER AND MORE LASTING IS THE JOY OF A PERSON WHO IS SET FREE FROM THE ETERNAL PUNISHMENT OF HIS SIN THROUGH ACCEPTING JESUS CHRIST AS SAVIOR. THERE IS NO HAPPIER STATE IN LIFE THAN TO BE PARDONED AND SET FREE ESPECIALLY WHEN YOU KNOW THAT YOU HAVE DONE NOTHING TO DESERVE IT. HAVE YOU TOLD SOMEONE LATELY THAT THEY CAN FIND FREEDOM IN CHRIST?

Verse: *"It is for freedom that Christ has set us free. Stand firm, then, and do not let yourselves be burdened again by the yoke of slavery".*

(GALATIANS 5:1)

The Folly
of Wisdom

ear friends at FEBC,

Single, determined, hardworking, I was pursuing a promising business career. Everything seemed to be going well for me. I had all it took to be happy. But I was not. Inside me, there was that painful awareness of something that was missing, an emptiness, a longing for something I knew I had yet to find.

I devoured a lot of books to fill my insatiable search for life's meaning. I bumped into historical facts about Jesus. I knew Him merely as a historical figure who existed years ago and made a significant contribution to mankind.

> *"I had all it took to be happy. But I was not. Inside me, there was that painful awareness of something that was missing, an emptiness, a longing for something I knew I had yet to find."*

Yet, I wondered. Could it be that there was more that I needed to know about Him, the life He lived or the message He sought to impart than the knowledge these books had afforded me? There was always that nagging question in my mind.

It was a long, weary day. I just arrived home from work when I scanned through the radio dial, dying for some music to relax me, when I heard someone talking about Jesus. It grabbed my attention. He might have the answers needed. It was Rev. Chuck Swindoll of **Insight for Living** explaining the third chapter of John. I found his way of explaining

---

"The moment I said that prayer from my heart,
I knew a change had happened inside me."

---

things really interesting, so every evening after that, I always see to it that I tune in to DYFR of the Far East Broadcasting Company from 6:30 a.m. until midnight.

After a month of listening, I came to an eventful night that forever changed my life. I was listening alone in my room when Dr. Swindoll made an invitation to receive Jesus as Lord and Savior. I knew God was speaking to my heart. Jesus was real, as real as He was two thousand years ago. That night, I made a decision for Christ and prayed with Dr. Swindoll.

The moment I said that prayer from my heart, I knew a change had happened inside me. I found what I had been longing for. I had just crossed over from death to life. I felt so happy.

The following day, I hurried to the Southern Baptist Church just across our house and shared my experience with the pastor, who lovingly accepted me into the church. I was baptized three months later, and everyday after that I've grown to love the Lord. It had not been an easy decision for me. My family and friends were radically against my newfound faith.

But I knew that I found something that was worth more than all the treasures on earth. I found the Lord and I would stand against all the oppositions. I've found the ministry of DYFR-FM helpful, too, in discipling me. It has provided me with rich spiritual insights, and guided me with the right doctrine and developed in me a deeper knowledge of and love for God. For the past twelve years, I have consistently been listening to DYFR, everyday before and after work. I have almost 85 *Insight for Living* Study Guides in my library now and I'm sharing some of them with some friends. I give a monthly pledge, and say a prayer daily for you in the radio ministry. I believe it's not easy work for you to be talking alone in that "box." But you are not actually alone.

You are talking to many and you are talking to one. What you are saying is making a difference in their lives.

In Christ,
Michael

PEOPLE WHO ARE SEEKING THE LORD USING ONLY THEIR INTELLECT USUALLY FIND IT DIFFICULT TO KNOW HIM. TO KNOW CHRIST IS NOT MERELY PUTTING FACTS INTO ONE'S HEAD. IT IS TO EXPERIENCE HIM AS A PERSON FOR HE TRULY LONGS FOR A PERSONAL RELATIONSHIP WITH HIS CHILDREN. IT IS TO SEE HIM IN THE DAY TO DAY AFFAIRS OF LIFE AS A FRIEND AND MASTER. THE SCIENTIST, BLAISE PASCAL, SAID THERE IS A GOD-SHAPED VACUUM IN THE HEART OF MAN THAT CAN ONLY BE FILLED BY GOD HIMSELF. HAVE YOU ASKED CHRIST TO FILL YOUR MIND AND LIFE WITH HIS PRESENCE AND REALITY?

Verse: *"But God chose the foolish things of the world to shame the wise; God chose the weak things of the world to shame the strong."*
(*I CORINTHIANS 1:27*)

Healed in Body and Soul

O n August 14, 1996, Mrs. Leticia delos Santos visited FEBC's station DXAS in Zamboanga City bringing two hens. This was her love offering to God and to the staff of the radio station and her way of thanking the Lord for the blessings she enjoyed daily ever since she and her family have become listeners to the radio programs. This is the inspiring testimony of her family.

Leticia and her husband Felicito have five children who are now in their twenties. They own a small farm of coconut trees and rice. The delos Santos family live in Sibuguey, Siay, Zamboanga del Sur, an island so remote that it takes them five hours to travel by motorboat and bus to get to the city. There are no television sets in Sibuguey. Newspaper men have never tried to visit this island, so radio is the only window they have to the outside world and their only source of information.

A listener to DXAS broadcasts in Zamboanga City.

The delos Santos family were Roman Catholics. However, Felicito, the head of the family, was not religious at all. In fact, he was against his family going to any church and he even despised all forms of religious practice.

Despite this attitude of Felicito, the family would tune in to DXAS and listen to the different radio programs.

In 1981, Felicito got very sick. He experienced a lot of pain and bleeding during bowel movements. For sometime, he suffered tremendously because of this illness to the point of fear.

In his desperation to find relief from his ailment Felicito began listening to the radio programs. Since a lot of prayers were said by pastors for the healing, salvation of listeners, he decided to join in the prayers. One day as he reached out in faith and touched his radio set while praying with the pastor on air, he experienced God's instant healing at that moment.

Convinced that it was the Lord Jesus Christ who healed him, Felicito immediately invited the pastor of a nearby church to hold a Bible study in their home. After continued Bible studies and listening to the broadcasts, the whole family became followers of the Lord Jesus Christ. Now, their eldest daughter is married to a pastor and their 23 year old son has been pastoring the Culuran One Way Church in Zamboanga del Sur.

PRAYER IS THE CHANNEL BY WHICH GOD RELEASES HIS BLESSINGS UPON OUR LIVES. THE LORD EVEN USES RADIO TO BRING HEALING TO THOSE WHO ARE SICK. HE CAN CHOOSE TO USE ANY MEANS AT ANY TIME AND ANY PLACE TO MAKE US WELL. HOWEVER, WE NEED TO BE FULLY YIELDED TO HIS WILL AND HIS TIMETABLE FOR HIM TO INDEED GET THE GLORY. WHAT PRAYERS HAS THE LORD ANSWERED IN YOUR LIFE FOR WHICH YOU WANT TO PRAISE HIM?

Verse: *"And I will do whatever you ask in my name, so that the Son may bring glory to the Father."* (JOHN 14:13)

From a Russian with Love

*T*he coin, with the Czar's head, was minted somewhere in Russia. By routes and persons unknown, it found its way to China. There, a young Christian couple was preparing to leave for a new life in Australia. Sometime after joining the more than 140,000 Russians at the time in Australia, the husband died suddenly. The wife was left caring for two young children while expecting a third. She plunged into despair.

After hearing FEBC's broadcasts in 1969, the young widow began writing Jack and Vera Koziol, Russian broadcasters in FEBC Philippines. She expressed concern for her countrymen in Australia, separated from their homeland by thousands of miles and their new neighbors by language and culture.

She started visiting Russians in her community, inviting them to listen to FEBC. They began asking about spiritual matters. The young widow didn't always have the answers. She regularly wrote the Koziols in Manila for help. Jack's reply included carefully chosen literature. The widow began to mature spiritually. Her enthusiasm infected others. Many listeners were moved. They wanted to know more about the Lord. Jack sent 20 Russian Bibles. The radio listeners who received them from the widow were elated. But many of them, because of their age, found it difficult to read the small print. Another call for help. Jack sent 20 large-print Bibles.

The widow's delight was inexpressible. She searched for a way to express her gratitude.

The long hidden gold coin came to mind- the coin with the Czar's head. This is her letter to Jack (Jacob) Koziol:

"Dear Brother Jacob and Sister Vera,

I thank you for the 20 small Bibles and the 20 large-print Bibles. I have distributed them all. I would like to repay you for them.

I am sending you a ten ruble Russian gold piece. I tremble as I send it. I had never seen gold before but when we were ready to leave China a man of the Tartar nationality brought in this pure gold piece to us. When we left China we sold a cow and a home to get this money. My husband and I had never seen this kind of money before so we did not know the value on it. We thought it was brass...then later read "pure gold" written on it.

He sold it to us for 500 rubles so we bought it. We thought we would use it if an emergency arose.

After my husband died, I lived in such grief and felt I was forgotten by all. I needed the money and wanted to sell it but did not know where to turn to do so.

Therefore God has put it in my heart to send it to you, dear brother Jacob. Please write and let me know if it comes to the total value of 100 rubles and will pay for the 20 Bibles you sent me. And you, dear brother Jacob, are not to write anymore that I "ought not to pay for the Bibles". I also want to share in the work and blessings of the Lord.

I give my last coin to the Lord.

Sister Anna"

When Jacob Koziol opened a package addressed to him, he could not believe what he saw. Not only was the gold coin in a box but it had a white cloth sewn around it. Along with the coin was Anna's testimony.

It was several weeks before Jack could freely share this testimony and display the gift. The message was too sacred to talk about in any light manner. The Widow's Best! What a challenge! She gave her last coin...from a Russian with love.

THE OBJECTS OF AFFECTION THAT WE TREASURE MOST IN THIS LIFE ARE THOSE THAT WE CANNOT LIVE WITHOUT. FOR SOME IT MAY BE A HOUSE, WEALTH, A PERSON OR EVEN A PROFESSIONAL CAREER. IF WE SUBMIT OUR TREASURES TO THE LORD AND FIND IN HIM OUR MOST PRECIOUS POSSESSION, THEN WE WILL EXPERIENCE JOY BEYOND COMPARE SPECIALLY IF WE HAVE GIVEN ALL THAT IS FLEETING IN THIS LIFE OVER TO OUR BELOVED MASTER. WHAT TREASURES ARE YOU KEEPING FOR YOURSELF OR GIVING AWAY FOR GOD'S SERVICE?

Verse: *"But store up for yourselves treasures in heaven, where moth and rust do not destroy and where thieves do not break in and steal. For where your treasure is, there your heart will be also."* (MATTHEW 6:20-21)

Hope for a Hurting Marriage

he following account is the story of one of FEBC's listeners who wishes to remain anonymous. We'll call her Glenda.

Glenda had been married nine years before she became a born-again Christian. However, she and her husband did not have a baby so they consulted with many doctors and tried almost everything just to have a baby. They prayed to all the patron saints they knew, pleading, even begging for a child. Nothing happened.

One day a friend told Glenda to pray only to the Lord Jesus Christ. That is what she did. She became a born-again Christian and turned from her former ways, living to please the Lord. God heard her prayers and in 1981, a year after she became a Christian, God blessed them with a son.

"Because of her husband's taking drugs, he began to abuse her nightly with beatings. She was so scarred emotionally and physically that she did not know whom to turn to."

Hungry to know more about God, Glenda read her Bible everyday and sought for a radio program that would feed her spiritually. One day, she accidentally found DZAS on her radio dial. The programs helped her in her Christian walk along with her regular fellowship with believers in church.

> *"Some of her relatives would advise her to separate from her husband but she followed the Lord's admonition that no man could separate what God had joined together. "*

But this was the beginning of her trials in her married life. She thought that having a child would improve their marriage, but it only got worse. Her husband spent more time with his *barkada* (gangmates) and became short-tempered. He began to forbid his wife from going to church because he was afraid that she would give all their money to the church.

She tried to share the Gospel with him on several occasions but he did not want to listen. He even told her to stop reading the Bible and listening to DZAS. Despondent, Glenda did not know what to do since the programs had become a great source of spiritual strength for her.

To make matters worse, after three children had been added to the family, her husband became a drug user. Life became increasingly bleak and dreary as her drugged husband began to abuse her nightly with beatings. She was so scarred emotionally and physically that she did not know what to do or whom to turn to.

A ray of hope came to her life when she bought a Walkman which enabled her to listen to the DZAS broadcasts at home. The programs, which brought her God's Word, became her source of strength throughout all her trials. She steadfastly held on to the Lord's promise that He would never abandon her. She would always remember Romans 8:28 and the truth she learned from the radio that all her trials served a purpose.

For 14 years, Glenda fervently prayed for the salvation of her husband, until one day, to her surprise, she found him listening to Chuck Swindoll's **Insight for Living** on DZAS. Her husband began to change. Finally, in 1995 after listening regularly to **Insight for Living**, he accepted the Jesus Christ as his Savior and Lord.

Today Glenda's family members are growing spiritually and serving the Lord together. She praises God and thanks Him for His goodness in their life. She testifies what a great help the radio programs had been to her especially during those times when she had no one to turn to.

"Were it not for you on the radio reminding me of the Lord's goodness, I probably would have committed suicide or would be in a mental institution today," she relates. Praise God that in Him we can, indeed, find hope even for those who have hurting marriages.

IT IS SAID THAT THE NEXT THING NEAREST TO HEAVEN IS A HAPPY HOME WHERE THE FAMILY MEMBERS LOVE ONE ANOTHER AND THE LORD. BUT SATAN WILL DO EVERYTHING IN HIS POWER TO DESTROY THE HOME WHICH HAS BEEN ORDAINED BY GOD. IT IS ONLY AS WE SUBMIT OURSELVES TO THE LORDSHIP OF CHRIST AND FOLLOW HIS WORD UNCOMPROMISINGLY THAT WE WILL HAVE THE VICTORY TO HAVE A GOD- HONORING HOME. IN WHAT WAYS ARE YOU PLEASING THE LORD AS A FAMILY?

Verse: *"Unless the Lord builds the house, its builders labor in vain."*
(PSALM 127:1A)

Story 30

Fighting no More

For many decades, Vietnam was a war-torn and terror-stricken land. Communists and the Saigon government with the Americans fought heavily on its soil. Thousands of people perished and hundreds more were left injured.

In the fifties, the Degas tribespeople staged a revolt against the Saigon government. In the sixties, however, they joined forces with Saigon and the American Green Berets to fight against the communist forces from the North. In 1984, the Degas decided to stop fighting.

"It has been a life of bitter struggle and hardship for these people. The one thing that keeps them going is their staunch faith in God—the Christian God."

The Degas were an oppressed people. They constantly struggled for their rights and autonomy. Amidst these struggles, who could give them hope?

FEBC started its tribal broadcasts to Vietnam in the early sixties when the Degas started fighting for their independence. We did not hear much from listeners, if there were any, because it was very difficult at that time for people in the hill countries of Vietnam to mail letters to the outside world. Our programmers only trusted God...that He would use the broadcasts to fill each listener's need.

It was in 1985, after more than 20 years of broadcasting, that the Lord strengthened and encouraged us with an unexpected glimpse of the fruit of these broadcasts.

We came across articles in *Asiaweek* which mentioned that our broadcasts have helped a beleaguered group of people. Here are some excerpts:

In the November 15, 1985 issue, a news item reads in part:

In September 1982, the Vietnamese government publicized the arrest and defection of several leaders of Montagnard hillfolk in the country's Central Highlands. The apparent motive: to imply that the rebel FULRO-Degas Movement, led by the Montagnards... no longer represented a credible force... Recently, some 200 Degas crossed into Thailand, seeking autonomy for its people....

The Degas told Thai authorities that they had kept their hopes alive by listening to regular radio broadcasts in their language from the Philippine-based Far East Broadcasting Company.

There was another article entitled "Ceasefire in Cloudland," in the December 6, 1986 issue of *Asiaweek* which traces the history of the political struggle of these tribal people—from the time they settled in

Believers from the Degas tribe of Northern Vietnam.

the mountain regions of Vietnam more than 2,000 years ago to the story of how 200 of them came to Thailand seeking to be resettled in a third country.

It has been a life of bitter struggle and hardship for these people. The one thing that has kept them going is their staunch faith in God— the Christian God. Most of the million or more Degas are Christians. They do not have a pastor but they manage.

The *Asiaweek* article said, *"There's also comfort in Dega/Rhade programs from the Christian funded Far East Broadcasting Company in the Philippines."*

Imagine! The Degas have been listening all that time, drawing comfort and assurance from God's Word uttered by broadcasters in the Philippines.

WHEN CHRIST CALLS US TO BE HIS FOLLOWERS, HE REQUIRES THAT WE LEAVE OUR OLD LIFESTYLE. JUST AS HE HAS CALLED THE FISHERMEN TO BE HIS DISCIPLES, SO HE ALSO CALLS US. SOME OF US MAY HAVE TO LEAVE OUR CAREERS, PLACES OF WORK, SINFUL PRACTICES AND HABITS, UNGODLY PEERS OR IDOLS THAT WOULD KEEP US FROM ENJOYING THE FULLNESS OF LIFE HE OFFERS. YOU WILL NEVER REGRET YOUR DECISION TO FOLLOW HIM. WHAT IS GOD IMPRESSING UPON YOU TO CHANGE IN ORDER TO FOLLOW HIM?

Verse: *Then Jesus said to His disciples, "If anyone would come after Me. He must deny himself and take up his cross and follow Me."*
(MATTHEW 16:24)

Story 31   Seeker of Truth

or ten years I lived without God. I lived a life without direction, fighting against self and the government.

It was not always that way. I grew up in a home that had religion. In fact, I was enrolled in a seminary at a young age. I thought I had a vocation for the priesthood, a call to serve. At an early age I often wondered about the meaning of life.

However, instead of going to seminary, I decided to become a medical doctor. I enrolled in a university at a time when student activism was rampant. Because I desired change, I joined the activist movement.

At first I didn't want violence so I joined the more moderate Social Democratic Movement. When nothing drastic happened I got impatient. I really wanted drastic change. First of all, I wanted to see change in my family that was beset by a lot of problems. I wanted to see radical changes in our society, in our economic and social structure.

As nothing was happening through the moderate groups, it was easy for me to accept the Communist doctrine and the armed revolution it espoused. I left my studies, my family, everything, and dedicated my whole life to the cause of Communism. I thought real meaning in life could be found by serving my country unselfishly

Soon, I lost faith in God. I began to believe that religion was only an opiate that made people blind to their miseries and the injustices around them.

Soon after martial law was declared in the Philippines, I joined the armed rebels in the mountains. As a Communist who was not afraid to die, I accepted the challenge of serving the movement, of being exposed to death, diseases, hunger and possible captivity. I served the Communist Party until I was arrested. For almost a year I was a political prisoner. But imprisonment did not reform me.

When I got out of prison, I saw the Communist movement with new eyes. I saw the human weakness... the senseless killing. Even in the highest leadership, I saw the inadequacy of the human mind and human efforts to bring real change to self and society. So after my release I thought, "the answer is not in Communism. There could be no real change there. Where is the answer?"

I tried to find the answer in unrestricted pleasure— wine, women, forbidden drugs. I went to the States and lived there for a while hoping to find an answer to my quest. I found none. I came back to the Philippines empty, with no direction, no meaning in life.

I began to think perhaps, there is a god after all... perhaps the answer is in heaven. So I went back to religion. I went to church regularly and said my prayers faithfully, desperately. But God did not answer. Religion gave no answers. Then, I remembered listening to the newscasts of DZAS while I was in the mountain. I knew it was a religious station so I tuned in to it and started listening.

There were a lot of things I heard which I couldn't accept, a lot more I couldn't understand. But I listened for five months, each minute the station was on the air. I wanted so much to understand this God they were talking about, to really know if He was for real.

All this time my problems had been compounding. I felt my life disintegrating slowly. As I felt the weight of my problems paralyzing me, one night I decided to end it all by jumping over the Pasig River. But as I was thinking about this, a Scripture verse I heard on DZAS

I tried to find the answer in unrestricted pleasure— wine, women, forbidden drugs. I went to the States and lived there for a while hoping to find an answer to my quest. I found none. I came back to the Philippines empty, with no direction, no meaning in life.

tugged at my mind. "Come unto me all ye that labor and are heavy-laden and I will give you rest..." The five months of listening to God's Word over the radio bore fruit.

That night I held on to that promise of Jesus. I cried to God in utter exhaustion, "God, if you're real, help me... I feel overwhelmed by my problems. I feel worthless as dung...". That night I accepted Jesus Christ into my heart as my personal Savior... And for the first time in 28 years, I was able to truly rest all through the night.

Ever since that day the pieces in the jigsaw puzzle of my life began to fit together. Christ is the answer! Through the programs on DZAS I learned what it really meant to "accept Jesus as Savior." The night I let Him come into my heart, He not only gave me meaning and direction in life, He also changed me completely into a brand new man. Praise God!

- Giovanni del Rosario

MAN IS PLAGUED WITH TRYING TO FIND THE MEANING OF LIFE. EVER SINCE THE CREATION, HE HAS BEEN SEEKING FOR THAT WHICH WILL GIVE HIM DIRECTION. IT IS ONLY IN THE PERSON OF JESUS CHRIST THAT ULTIMATE MEANING CAN BE FOUND BECAUSE HE IS THE LIFE GIVER. IN WHAT WAYS HAVE YOU SOUGHT FOR MEANING IN YOUR LIFE?

Verse: Jesus said: *"I come that they may have life and might have it abundantly."* (JOHN 10:10)

God's Leading and *Lahar*

*I*n 1996, we received a unique feedback for **Heartline**, a counseling program on station DZAS. The listener shared some pages from his personal journal. Let's take a peek into the personal life of this listener, Rey M. Reyes.

September 30, 1995 - A strong typhoon was coming through our town. It was a Saturday. In spite of the typhoon, I was excited to go to church and we were praising the Lord.

A house and vehicle half-buried in lahar.

9:00 a.m. October 1 - The *lahar** in our town of San Fernando, Pampanga came down.

9:10 a.m. October 1 - We lost everything - our home, our business, our clothes and possessions. (Everything

*Mud flows from the volcanic eruption of Mount Pinatubo

was buried by the *lahar*). All of us in the family were on top of our roof - without water and food for 24 hours. All I could hear were the cries and screams of those around me. *"Kawawa po silang lahat at napakaraming namatay sa aming lugar"* (they were all pitiful and a lot of people died at our place).

I could not do anything for them except pray. A lot of questions came into my mind. I did not want to ask why because I knew that God knew what we were going through. I said: "Lord I don't know what your purpose is in all of this but I trust in You."

October 2-5 - It's only now that I feel the responsibility of being the eldest in my family. My mother and father are in a state of shock. The rest of our family has gone to my father's best friend in Bulacan. I have been left here to keep watch on our rooftop because there were thieves who stole our things inside the house, even the clothes that are full of mud.

October 6 - Looking at my family, I felt hopelessness and despair. *"Malapit na akong bumigay sa aking buhay pananampalataya"* (I almost lost all hope in my Christian faith). I was the only Christian then in our family. All I could do was cry out to the Lord until I saw a radio in the house we were staying and I tuned in to DZAS.

The program at that time was **Heartline** and the topic was on trials. The counselor said, "Sometimes we don't know why some things happen to us but God is there to guide us. Don't quit, friend, God is in you." When I heard these words it seemed like I was able to stand again as if with the renewed wings of the eagle! Had it not been for DZAS being used to bring me the Word of the Lord, where would I be today?

That moment I said, "Lord, you really have a purpose for my life. Please use me in this place." It was also on that day that I decided to follow the Lord's calling to enter His ministry. I saw His calling upon my life and that burden grew in my heart.

He led me to a church where I could fellowship with believers and serve Him. Praise the Lord that I was able to bring my cousins and whole family there and now they have accepted the Lord Jesus as their

Savior. Now I am a pastor at Jesus Christ the Redeemer Church in Pulilan, Bulacan. Praise God for using your station's **Heartline** program to speak to me. All my tears and prayers have not been in vain.

THERE ARE INSTANCES WHEN GOD SPEAKS TO US THROUGH THE TRIALS AND PROBLEMS HE SENDS OUR WAY. IT IS IN THE FURNACE THAT WE CAN GET TO KNOW HIM AND EXPERIENCE HIM FOR ALL THAT HE IS. IT IS ALSO THROUGH THE FIRE THAT WE CAN GET TO SEE WHO WE REALLY ARE AND LEARN TO DEAL WITH OUR WEAKNESSES AND SINS. BUT GOD IS FAITHFUL FOR HE HAS PROMISED TO BE WITH US IN ALL THESE. WHAT LESSONS HAVE YOU LEARNED FROM THE LORD THROUGH THE TRIALS IN YOUR LIFE RIGHT NOW?

Verse: *"When you pass through the waters, I will be with you; and when you pass through the rivers, they will not sweep over you. When you walk through the fire, you will not be burned; the flames will not set you ablaze… Do not be afraid for I am with you."*

(ISAIAH 43:2 & 5)

New Life in Jail

My life was filled with hatred and revenge. Both my parents and one of my brothers were killed by the New People's Army (military men of the Communist Party of the Philippines). I joined a civilian defense group, the most notorious people in our place. We would beat anyone who stood in our way. And kill indiscriminately when we were drunk. I also became a drug user, and eventually, a drug pusher. We were on top of the government's "Wanted: Shoot to Kill" list. Finally, in January 1994, I was arrested.

It was inside the prison cell that my life started to change.

While I was in jail, people from different religious groups would visit us and hold Bible studies. I joined one of the groups. We learned songs and had some Bible sharing. But after the meetings, we'd get back to gambling, drinking.

"We would beat anyone who stood on our way. And kill indiscriminately when we were drunk. I also became a drug user, and eventually, a drug pusher. We were on top of the government's "Wanted: Shoot to Kill" list."

There was a group that caught my attention. Two ladies from a Christian radio station called DYFR (FEBC's station in Cebu City) led them. They were really different. They were happy. Oftentimes I would find them reading their Bible after their meeting. They must really be taking their bible studies seriously. The rest of us thought they were a bunch of weirdos— the "hallelujah-praise the Lord" people.

After a while, I started to join this group. I began to enjoy the Bible studies. Gina and Becky (the workers of DYFR) brought us portable missionary (PM) radios tuned in to station DYFR only.

On one of those ordinary days, I understood my true condition. A sinner who needed God. If I had to collect all my sins and put them all in a ship, there would be enough sins to sink it, but God's love was greater than the ocean. That day I turned my life over to Jesus and felt inside that peace that passes all understanding.

I was ridiculed and sometimes threatened by other inmates, but I kept on in my newfound faith and found God showing me more and more of His great love and power every day.

One of these monumental victories was the hearing on my case. I was arrested for illegal possession of firearms and might be sentenced to 17 years of imprisonment. But my fears were vanquished by God's promise. He showed me the verse Jeremiah 33:3, "Call unto me and I will answer you. And I will show you great and mighty things that you have not known."

Before the hearing, I was advised by my lawyer to deny the allegations. I was told to practice what to say during the interrogation. But it was against my conviction to lie. I did what I knew was right: I admitted the offense. Everyone was thinking I was abandoning myself to fate but in fact, I abandoned myself to God. I knew He would do as He has promised. To everyone's astonishment my case was dismissed.

Now, I'm regularly attending church. The hands I once used to bruise my wife when I was drunk are now hands I use to help her with the laundry. The tongue once used to say curses and the meanest of words is now used to tell others about the love of Christ. Everywhere I am, I tell people about God's love. I love the Lord. And I know it is because He first loved me. This love I got to know because of radio people who took the time to visit social outcasts like me to tell me God loved and valued me.

--Richard

No matter how vile or dirty our past may be we must always remember that our God is in the business of changing lives. That's what Christ came for— to bring us new life and set us free from the bondage of sin and death. What changes have the Lord brought into your life since you gave your life to Him?

Verse: *"Therefore if anyone is in Christ, he is a new creation; the old has gone , the new has come."* (2 Corinthians 5:17)

Story 34

Running Away from God

*T*his is the true story of *Ka* Cesar, who, in running away from everyone and everything, found that he could not run away from God.

During his senior year in high school, *Ka* Cesar (his pseudonym) gave his life to Christ. At that time, he didn't realize the implications of his commitment but an American missionary told him someday he would become a pastor. Let us trace his spiritual journey from being a student activist to the fulfillment of the American missionary's prophecy.

Once more Ka Cesar heard about the God who loved him and would never forsake him. He began to pray in his heart, "Lord, please get me out of here and one day I will serve You".

While in college, *Ka* Cesar and his twin brother were branded as Communists because of their participation in the student movement in the 70's. They sponsored and translated a play called "The East is Red" while joining street rallies and demonstrations. A lot of these activities were attributed to youthful idealism.

One day, some student leaders told *Ka* Cesar to turn on his television to the evening news. To his surprise and fear, he saw among the headlines that he and his brother were to be arrested by the government. Immediately, he went into hiding, seeking refuge with friends who networked with the underground New People's Army (NPA), the military arm of the Communist Party of the Philippines. It was Christmas Eve.

Ka Cesar was taken to a safehouse in Baguio City. That Christmas Eve, the radio was playing Christmas music, tuned to FEBC. Once again, *Ka* Cesar heard about the love of God for him. It brought back a lot of memories of his high school conversion and caused him to ask himself why he got into this situation. He felt like a pawn used for the political purposes of the NPA and there was no escape from it.

His life was not easy in the safehouse although it seemed exciting at first. When he requested some personal items like clothes and a Bible from his brother, his comrades said, "Burn the Bible. We don't need it here." Daily, they would study Mao's red book and discuss it like having a Bible study.

In the safehouse, *Ka* Cesar's assignment was to listen to Radio Peking every morning to get the news, commentaries and teachings of Mao in Chinese and to translate these into the Pilipino language. Every morning, he would listen on his shortwave radio to a dose of Communist propaganda but there were times when he would tune in to the FEBC Chinese broadcasts.

He was searching and beginning to seriously question the meaning of life. And something inside kept beckoning him to listen to the Gospel over the radio. He said: "Somehow, I was looking for God but I didn't realize it was God seeking me through FEBC."

As he continued to listen, once more *Ka* Cesar heard about the God who loved him and would never forsake him. He began to pray in his heart, "Lord, please get me out of here and one day I will serve You."

His prayer was answered. One day, *Ka* Cesar had an urge to ask for a newspaper, something which they would not usually buy or read in the safehouse. Surprisingly, his comrades granted his request. As he flipped through the pages of the newspaper, he was shocked to read on the obituary page that his beloved mother had died a few days earlier in a vehicular accident in Hong Kong. After pleading with his companions, *Ka* Cesar was able to go to Manila and verify his mother's death.

His mother's death and the callous way his NPA comrades treated his moment of tragedy brought *Ka* Cesar to a turning point in his involvement with Communism. From that moment on, he began to plot his escape. He said, "I was running away from everybody: from the Chinese community, the Philippine government and the NPA".

Not too long after, he and his twin brother made a dramatic escape to Hong Kong and broke away from the movement. *Ka* Cesar went to the U.S. and, through a series of miraculous interventions, the Lord led him to a church in California. This time *Ka* Cesar really meant business with God. During one of the church services, he recommitted his life to the Lord Jesus Christ. He was no longer running away from God.

Today *Ka* Cesar is faithfully serving the Lord as a pastor in a church in the U.S., a living proof that God is the God of second chances. FEBC President Carlos Peña even met him personally.

HAVE YOU EVER EXPERIENCED RECEIVING A SECOND CHANCE IN LIFE? OUR LORD IS THE GOD OF SECOND CHANCES— HE GIVES OPPORTUNITIES TO PEOPLE TIME AND AGAIN TO COME TO HIM IN REPENTANCE. IN THE BIBLE, WE ENCOUNTER SEVERAL PEOPLE TO WHOM GOD GAVE A SECOND CHANCE: JONAH, PETER, JACOB, TO NAME A FEW. CAN YOUR NAME BE ADDED TO THIS LIST? DON'T DELAY TO RETURN TO HIM!

Verse: *"He is patient with you, not wanting anyone to perish, but everyone to come to repentance."* (2 PETER 3:9)

Why My Life was Spared

$\mathcal{T}$he following is based on the true story of an FEBC listener in Cambodia.

The picture is indelibly printed on my mind. Thoughts and questions raced through it. I was confronted by what seemed inevitably to be the last moments of my life.

Death.

What had I done to deserve death at such a young age? And who were they to condemn me anyhow? Murderers!

Was this really the end? My mind worked feverishly. Was escape at all possible?

Cambodians listening to the radio.

Suddenly a piercing scream arrested my thoughts. An ax fell. A head rolled and lay silent in the deep pit before me. It was my friend's. And I was next.

"It's worth a try," I told myself. Courage suddenly welled up within from some hidden resource.

I attracted the attention of one of the executioners.

"Could I be allowed to die with my hands untied?" I was desperate at this point.

To my amazement, they granted my wish. As the rope fell to the ground I grabbed the man with the machete and wrapped an arm around his neck. There was no time to lose. Snatching the weapon from his hand I shoved the muzzle against his neck, then backed away from the others using my captive to shield me from their rifles.

Reaching the jungle's edge, I shoved the man to the ground, and fled. Looking for cover, I found a haystack nearby and dived into it. But though they searched, they couldn't find me.

Now, this was not my first experience with the Communist Khmer Rouge. They had taken away father, a former senator in the ousted Lon Nol government, to work in a communal where, because of the hard labor and lack of food, he finally died.

My mother was taken to another province to work in the fields, and I have not heard of her since.

My own personal encounter with the Khmer Rouge, which I have just described, began as a work assignment with 2,000 other young people about my age (I was in my third year of college when the Communists took over my country).

We were given the job of digging 5' x 5' pits to be used in storing buffalo and horse manure. At least, that's what we were told.

Little did we realize it was for our own burial.

> *"It is hard to describe feelings when one has had two such close brushes with death. I did not want to die - I had my whole life ahead of me."*

Each pit was made to hold five bodies. Four of my friends worked alongside me, and finally when the hole was dug, we were ordered to sit down by the pit. Then our hands were tied behind our backs. Our crimes were that we had done something against the government and high officials, so we were informed.

One by one my friends were brutally murdered. I alone was able to escape. But my freedom was not to last for long. I returned to my hometown, and people there gladly took me in because they could see I was sick. But the Khmer Rouge came again and evacuated both young and old, putting us on two boats to "transport" us to a different area. As the first boat reached land it struck a mine. The violent explosion killed outright everyone aboard.

I was in the second boat, awaiting a similar fate as soon as we reached shore. But then the miraculous happened. The Vietnamese offensive had just reached into that area, and the Khmer Rouge fled before they were able to blow up our boat. As a result, my life was spared a second time.

It is hard to describe feelings when one has had two such close brushes with death. I did not want to die. I had my whole life ahead of me. And felt as though I did not yet know the meaning of my existence. Moreover, I was afraid of what lay beyond death's door.

Things got a little better for my family and me after the Vietnamese took over our country. We were able to plant crops and barter goods, which had been impossible before.

I even obtained enough gold to buy a radio and listened every night to the Voice of America. One evening I happened by accident to tune to a Christian broadcast from FEBC in Manila. I believe God truly opened my heart through this encounter, for I became very much interested in Christianity.

I was also preoccupied with my desire to get out of the country as quickly as possible. I had enough gold left to bribe the Vietnamese for a passage by army car to the province of Battambang. From there I escaped to Thailand. From Thailand I got to the Philippines by plane.

Now I know why my life was spared two times in Cambodia. I arrived in Morong, Bataan February 5, 1980. The next day I met a Cambodian lady who worked in FEBC Manila, and the following day she led me to the Lord. Praise God!

YOU ARE HERE FOR A PURPOSE AND THOUGH YOU FEEL YOU MAY NOT KNOW IT YET, GOD WILL SHOW THIS TO YOU STEP BY STEP. YES, THE LORD HAS A PLAN FOR YOUR LIFE BUT YOU NEED TO LEARN TO YIELD YOURSELF TO HIS WILL AND TRUST HIS GUIDANCE IN YOUR LIFE. ARE YOU READY TO COME TO HIM IN FAITH AND FOLLOW HIS CALL IN YOUR LIFE?

Verse: *"And we know that in all things God works for the good of those who love Him, who have been called according to His purpose."*
- (ROMANS 8:28)

Story 36 — God's Gardener

*T*he clock strikes 5:30 a.m. and *Hardin ng Panalangin's* (Garden of Prayer) theme music is up, then the familiar and well-loved voice of Pastor Proceso Marcelo is heard.

"*Ang pangarap ko noon ay makapasok sa NBI [National Bureau of Investigation] dahil ang paborito kong suot ay pantalon na khaki, trobinized na puti na nakaliles ang manggas. Mayroong kalibre .45 na baril sa baywang at may dalang jacket kahit na tanghaling tapat. Kaya lang binago ng Panginoon [ang lahat]. Sa halip na sa NBI dinala [Niya] ako sa BBI [Bethel Bible Institute]* (My wish then was to work at the NBI because my favorite outfit were khaki trousers, shirts with long sleeves folded, a .45 caliber gun tucked on my waistband and a jacket on my arm even when it's hot. But the Lord changed all that. Instead of the NBI, He brought me to BBI)," quips FEBC Evangelist-at-large Pastor Marcelo.

> "His fondest wish to be an NBI agent did not come true, but in God he received so much more than he'd ever dreamed."

Pastor Marcelo or *Ka* Esong, as he is known among the staff and close friends, has been with FEBC for 50 years. He inspires many. This was not always so.

At 14, during World War II, he joined the Rey-Zar regiment guerrilla group and delivered messages from camp to camp. It was dangerous but he was unfazed. When the Americans arrived, he joined the American Allied forces enabling him to see action in Lucena, Quezon and Batangas.

Though the war ravaged the country's economy, *Ka* Esong seemed unscathed by poverty. He impressed his mother whenever he dutifully turned over his pay envelope to her— his salary intact. She was unaware that he was stowing under the pillow bounties from illegal activities.

Upon his father's death, he went from bad to worse. But his mother, a deeply religious woman, never gave up on him. Once she asked his older brother Jose to take *Ka* Esong to FEBC for employment.

FEBC initially took him in for two weeks.

Rev. Proceso Marcelo preaching during the program "Hardin ng Panalangin" (Garden of Prayer) aired daily for over 40 years now.

He helped in the construction of office and transmitter buildings, roads and houses, and collected garbage.

John Broger, one of FEBC's co-founders, required *Ka* Esong and his co-workers to attend a daily Bible study under Max Atienza. Before the study of John chapter three was over *Ka* Esong repented of his old life and became a Christian.

He joyfully shared his faith with his mother. To his consternation she accused him of being drunk or crazy. But he persisted. One day he told her that he was keen on going to Bible school to learn how to effectively share the Gospel with her. This revelation convinced her that he was serious.

So off he went to Bible school. But life was not easy. *Ka* Esong scrimped, saved and walked the four kilometers to school and back. He was gate guard for seven years, many times working on the 5:00 p.m. to 1:00 a.m. shift.

Once in a while he would be involved in DZAS radio productions as voice talent. One thing led to another. *Ka* Esong was then assigned as a news correspondent to the Malacañang beat.

One day he noticed barrels of unread telegrams at the Press Secretary's Office. It was a practice of then President Magsaysay to encourage the people to send him a telegram free of charge. It amazed him that people did this believing their problems would be heard by the President. Thus *Hardin ng Panalangin* was born, with the promise that all prayer requests listeners send in will surely be prayed for. From the initial 15 minutes the program now runs for one hour daily.

Today Ka Esong is way, way off his unscrupulous beginnings. His fondest wish to be an NBI agent did not come true, but in God he received so much more than he'd ever dreamed.

JESUS COMPARED OUR LIVES TO BRANCHES THAT ARE CONNECTED TO HIM, THE VINE. HE HAS CHOSEN EACH CHRISTIAN FOR A PURPOSE. AND THAT IS TO BRING FORTH MUCH FRUIT FOR HIS GLORY. AS THE GARDENER, GOD THE FATHER PRUNES US THROUGH TRIALS AND TRIBULATIONS, SO WE COULD BE MORE FRUITFUL IN HIS GARDEN. IN WHAT WAYS ARE YOU YIELDING YOURSELF TO THE TOUCH OF OUR MASTER GARDENER?

Verse: *Jesus said "You did not choose me, but I chose you and appointed you to go and bear fruit - fruit that will last..."* (JOHN 15:16)

Widow's Mite: 20th Century Version

One cold morning I (Awit Castillo*) caught sight of an elderly lady standing patiently under a mango tree in the FEBC compound. I stopped to talk with her, and led her to the office. She introduced herself as Mrs. Martha S. Quitolbo, a 73-year old widow. She came to bring her love gift to FEBC. Braving the chilly December breeze which aggravated her rheumatism, she came herself to make sure that her Lord's money was surrendered first thing in the morning. Later, at eight o'clock, she had to report to work. Mrs. Quitolbo is not a regular employee working in any plush office; she is a laundry woman washing clothes for a family three times a week, earning P8.00 ($1.00 at that time) a day. Although her body is weakly aging with her years, her spiritual stamina and devotion to the Lord drive her to spend her years in sacrifice and hard work.

"My gift to FEBC is really for my Lord, but ah, it's lost!"

That morning of December 22, 1975, she tucked P100.00 in her brassiere, typical of Filipino old folk's way of keeping money in supposedly sure safety. She was on

* Former FEBC staff writer

her way to the FEBC compound. She just wanted to make sure that her money wouldn't be stolen from her, she explained, as she started to shake loose her bra. Suddenly, I saw in her face signs of bewilderment. She became increasingly distressed as signs of loss became evident. After much futile searching, with my assistance, she sighed in deep anguish, "Oh, I lost my Lord's money!" I empathized with her when between sobs and sighs, she told me her story.

Everyday, during the past several months, she had set aside 20 centavos from her wage so that she could give something to the Lord on Christmas day. Since 1949, she continued, "I have been greatly blessed by the ministry of FEBC. I always supplement my prayers with tangible amounts each year. My gift to FEBC is really for my Lord, but ah, it's lost!" Soon after, she bade me goodbye to catch up with her work, but not before she had promised to work even harder to 'repay', as she puts it, her Lord's money. And work, she did! Two weeks later, she came back to FEBC with the 'replacement'.

Mrs. Quitolbo's testimony was shared by our former Director Fred Rev. Magbanua on his daily program, **FEBC Insight**. Barely two weeks after its airing, a high school girl who heard it sent this letter to us:

"I was deeply touched by your interview with the laundry woman who lost the money she saved for the Lord, intended for FEBC. I was greatly challenged how she could give despite her poverty. My love for the Lord caught on new fire, and my interest in the ministry of the Far East Broadcasting Company was heightened. More than ever, I saw the great role you are playing in the spiritual ministry around the world. I am a prayer warrior of FEBC, and I have always thought that my prayers would suffice.....Recently our school choir had a performance. I am the pianist of the group, and accompanist. I am sending this money to help the ministry of FEBC of winning souls. Rest assured of my prayers....."

The widow's mite in the New Testament was not much. The mite of the widow, Mrs. Quitolbo, was not much either. But little is much when God is in it.

OUR LORD JESUS DOES NOT LOOK AT THE AMOUNT WE GIVE, BUT AT THE HEART OF THE GIVER. DIFFERENT PEOPLE GIVE OUT OF DIFFERENT MOTIVES. SOME GIVE TO BE RECOGNIZED; OTHERS, THAT THEIR NAMES BE PERPETUATED IN STONE. BUT GOD IS NOT IMPRESSED WITH SUCH GIVERS. THE JOYFUL AND CHEERFUL SPIRIT IS MUCH MORE VALUABLE TO THE LORD. THAT IS WHAT PLEASES HIM. ARE YOU GIVING TO THE LORD WITH A HAPPY HEART?

Verse: "Each man should give what he has decided in his heart to give, not reluctantly or under compulsion, for God loves a cheerful giver."
-(2 CORINTHIANS 9:7)

A Mother's Last Plea

*T*he following letter came to Jack Koziol, when he was FEBC's Director of Russian programming in Manila, Philippines in the seventies:

"Dear Brother in Christ,

I am not even worthy to call you a brother but I am doing this for the sake of my dear mother. At this time I must tell you the very sad news. I have lost my dear mother forever and forever. After her surgery she lived only five months. She was conscious up to the last minute of life. A week before she died she tried to speak to me, but I could not understand what she was saying, her tongue was so dry. She left us on June 22. I wanted her body kept in the home, but my children persuaded me against it because of my great grief. Oh, I feel as though I have lost my right eye, for I will remain blind forever. I will never see her again and I am not worthy to be called God's child. I caused my mother great heartache, for I never obeyed her, but chose to go contrary to her wishes.

> *"I caused my mother great heartache, for I never obeyed her, but chose to go contrary to her wishes."*

Now I ask you, could there be forgiveness of sins for such a person as I am? I am of no use to the Lord Jesus and not even to Satan, for what need would he have of me? I do not think the Lord God will ever forgive me.

My mother listened to your programs faithfully, and you wrote to her and sent her books so faithfully. I thank you for it."

Some time later, our listener wrote again:

"Peace be unto you, dear brother in Christ, Jacob Koziol:

I received your letter, for which I am very grateful to you. I thank you for your comfort and encouragement and good wishes for me. I was very despondent and I felt as though I was left alone. Now after receiving your letter I do not feel alone.

I have followed your teaching and have asked the Lord to forgive me. I believe He has forgiven me, as I have followed your instructions. I have joy and peace which I have not experienced in my life.

You sent many books to my mother. She begged me to read them, but I refused even to look at them. Now I am reading them with such great interest, and I cannot even explain why I am so fascinated by them and I do not feel so lonely now."

"For peace I had great bitterness: but Thou hast in love to my soul delivered it from the pit of corruption: for Thou hast cast all my sins behind Thy back" (Isaiah 38:17).

Praise God for His forgiveness, and that He has enabled us to share burdens like these with listeners in atheistic counties.

THANK GOD FOR PEOPLE WHO HAVE CARED FOR OUR SOUL DEEPLY ENOUGH TO PRAY FOR US. THERE ARE NO WORDS MORE COMFORTING TO HEAR THAN "I'M PRAYING FOR YOU." CHRISTIAN PARENTS, PARTICULARLY MOTHERS, POSSESS THAT SPECIAL GIFT OF SPIRITUAL DISCERNMENT AND PRAYERFULNESS WHEN IT COMES TO THEIR CHILDREN. BLESSED IS THE PERSON WHO HAS A PRAYING MOTHER. DO YOU HAVE CHRISTIAN PARENTS OR PEOPLE THAT YOU CAN THANK TODAY AS THEY STAND BY YOU IN PRAYER?

Verse: *"For this reason I kneel before the Father, from whom His whole family in heaven derives its name. I pray that out of His glorious riches He may strengthen you with power through His Spirit in your inner being."*
(EPHESIANS 3:14-16)

From Trials to Triumph

elson Bañez was the Vice President of a flourishing bank in Manila. When the bank closed down when martial law was declared, Nelson and some of his colleagues were arrested by the military and detained at a military camp. He was detained in June, 1974. Nine months after, in March, a fellow detainee introduced him to DZAS for "comfort and enlightenment." He became a regular listener of the station.

"He was detained in June, 1974. Nine months after, in March, a fellow detainee introduced him to DZAS for 'comfort and enlightenment.' "

Outside the camp Nelson's wife was undergoing mental and emotional anguish. She suffered much during the time that she was not informed of her husband's whereabouts. Faithful friends stood by her during moments of grief, particularly when she was hospitalized because of a nervous breakdown. These Christian friends took the opportunity to introduce Christ to her. Through their faithful witness and prayers, Eden received Christ as her personal Savior.

Those three months, though seemingly unending, passed by swiftly. Eden was finally informed of her husband's location and was allowed to visit him on weekends. Eden started sharing with her husband her new found faith and the gift of salvation in Christ.

Nelson saw the dramatic changes in Eden's life as a result of her conversion to Christ. This also contributed to his interest in what Christ can do to an individual.

He also saw Eden's unusual desire to talk to people about Christ and share her new found joy and happiness. Eden's transformed life was also instrumental in Nelson's conversion.

Nelson continued to listen to DZAS and read the Bible. One day in March, 1975, Nelson was alone in his room reading a booklet by Richard de Haan. After reading the literature, he recognized his true condition before God and his need for His forgiveness and salvation. Right then and there in his room he opened his heart to Christ and accepted Him as personal Savior.

After that Nelson wrote a long letter to FEBC to express his deep appreciation for its Bible programs. He also shared his ideas and opinions on life, religion and the world. He was grateful for FEBC's role in spreading the Gospel particularly in places where people do not have contact with the outside world— in prisons and detention centers.

Nelson started to pray very hard for his colleagues' and his own release. God answered this prayer on December 27, 1977. He was given an unconditional and absolute release by the President. The family reunion shortly before New Year was indescribable. Only the Lord who is able to deliver His children could know the joy that filled the heart of the Bañez family.

Soon after, he visited FEBC and offered his services. Since then, he has been serving God through the FEBC ministry in La Mirada, California.

WHEN THE BROKEN PIECES OF LIFE SEEM BEYOND REPAIR, DON'T GIVE UP! WE HAVE A WONDERFUL MASTER TO HELP PUT YOUR LIFE BACK TOGETHER AGAIN. YOU CAN ALWAYS COUNT ON HIM, EVEN THROUGH LIFE'S TRIALS AND DIFFICULTIES THAT HE WILL BRING ABOUT SOMETHING BEAUTIFUL FROM THE BROKEN PIECES IN YOUR LIFE. HOW HAS GOD USED THE BROKENNESS AND STRIFE IN YOUR LIFE TO COME UP WITH SOMETHING BEAUTIFUL?

Verse: "...We also rejoice in our sufferings, because we know that suffering produces perseverance; perseverance, character; and character, hope."
(ROMAN 5:3-4)

Excerpts from the Hmong Treasury

*F*or many years, we have received countless letters from the Hmong people of Laos and Thailand. Literacy rates in these countries are relatively higher than in Vietnam.

In 1991, startling information appeared in a Hanoi Sunday newspaper that referred to apparent mass Christianization of the Hmong of the Vietnam highlands. The article blamed this phenomenon on specific radio broadcasts from Manila.

Subsequent articles made further references to this phenomenon but it was in 1993 that we received the first communication from the Vietnamese Hmong themselves, which presented a "census" of 330,000 Christians! Contacts with the Vietnamese Minority Affairs confirmed that the government assesses the number of Christians to be around 250,000. While these statistics may pique one's interest, expressions from the Hmong themselves really touch the heart.

Here are a few excerpts from the Hmong treasury. Each one tells a unique story.

From Laos:

Praise the Lord! Four families including my own, have accepted the Lord Jesus Christ into our hearts.

Before I was an evil spirit worshipper and I was going insane. I thought that one day I would die and go to hell! But since I have heard your broadcast, I have been healed and turned normal again. Thank God.

We live very far from the city and have no contact with church leaders or other Christians. You're the only one we can count on.

From Vietnam:

How we thank you for your daily broadcast that is beamed over to us. God's words touch our hearts and give us encouragement to live another day.

Vietnamese article talking about Hmong becoming Christians.

Many people here do not write to thank you but your prayers have healed many people. I believe that these miracles occurred to show believers and unbelievers that only He can release our Hmong people from the bondage of Satan. Christ is the King of kings and Lord of lords.

Persecution is still going on but God's hand has protected us many times. Keep on broadcasting. We need your guidance to show us how to glorify our Father.

With these letters, we can have a glimpse of what God is doing in remote places hidden by jungles and mountainous terrain. This poem was recited by a Hmong on a cassette tape. Translated as closely as possible to its original form, his expression says it all:

I praise the Lord for the Gospel that comes my way.
I have been fighting myself sometimes that I have received better news than love.
It is so hard to fight myself and come to terms.
I sometimes see an evil that tends to keep me down.

I nearly died several times because I was in so hatred of my life and my
love.
After I heard about God's love and learned about Satan, I was in love
with Jesus.
I went to look for God, whether it was a rose or a beautiful person,
but I found God in my heart.
And this love was different.
So contagious like a wildfire I took the Lord's love into me.
From that instant my life changed.
Now I want to live and serve my family with God.

IMAGINE GOD'S BOUNDLESS JOY WHEN A SOUL TURNS FROM SIN,
AND HIS DEEP SORROW WHEN HE SEES PEOPLE WITHOUT A SAVIOR.
JESUS WAS MOVED TO COMPASSION WHEN HE SAW A CROWD WITHOUT
A SHEPHERD, WITHOUT DIRECTION AND PURPOSE IN LIFE. IT WAS NOT
SIMPLY PITY, BUT IT WAS COMPASSION THAT DROVE HIM TO DIE ON
CALVARY. WE NEED NOT DIE FOR THESE PEOPLE, BUT WE CAN GIVE OF
OUR LIVES FOR THEM IN SIMPLE ACTS OF LOVE AND CONCERN. IN
PRAYER, LET US ASK THE LORD HOW HE CAN USE US TO TOUCH OTHER
PEOPLE'S LIVES FOR HIS GLORY.

Verse: "In the same way, let your light shine before men, that they may
see your good deeds and praise your Father in heaven." (MATTHEW 5:16)

No More Walls

*A*lmost thirty years ago Shikha, who belonged to a high caste family in India, visited Malaysia and met Suba Passah, a low caste Hindu. During those days a high-caste Hindu must have no social interaction with one who is low born. But the friendship developed between Suba and Shikha deepened into love until finally, they got married against the wishes of Shikha's parents.

Feeling disgrace over the marriage of their daughter, Shikha's parents disowned her. Hurt, humiliated, she tried to commit suicide.

Then another crisis hit the family. Suba was stricken by a very serious ailment that caused him to leave his

A Hindu family in India

> *"Feeling disgrace over the marriage of their daughter, Shikha's parents disowned her. Hurt, humiliated, she tried to commit suicide."*

job. Worst of all, the doctors declared there was no chance that he could recover.

Almost at the end of her rope, she turned to her family for comfort and support.…. But they hardened their hearts. Her tears did not move them. She remained an outcast from her family.

This was more than she could bear. Death could not be worse than this, she thought. Amidst her turmoil, one night she turned on her radio. She heard strange and unfamiliar things. Hope… Love… The friendly voice said these things could be found in one Person, a personal God! Joy welled up from her heart as she listened to the voice telling her that the Son of God, Jesus Christ, loved her and gave His life for her.

She was listening to a program of the Far East Broadcasting Company coming from its studios in Metro Manila.

Because of that program, Shikha entrusted her life to the Lord. Later, one after another, her husband, son and daughter also came to know Jesus Christ as their Lord and Savior.

Shikha wrote to FEBC about her new-found joy and purpose in life. And about what God had done through FEBC. She also started sending in small gifts in appreciation for the blessings she had been receiving.

In the early eighties, Rev. Fred Magbanua, then FEBC Managing Director, visited this family in a rubber plantation in Malaysia where Shikha told him this story. And then, in an overwhelming demonstration of gratitude to God and the programs of FEBC, she gave two of her prized possessions: a gold ring and a gold pendant. She said, "I don't have much in worldly goods but I'd like to help the ministry. Sell these and use the money where most needed."

Today, the family continues to serve God in Malaysia and be His shining light in their little corner of the world.

A Malay who embraces the Christian faith, may lose his right as a citizen, including his right to hold a job. A believer who shares his faith risks imprisonment. New or actively witnessing Christians soon find themselves deserted by their families and friends. Persecuted and rejected, believers in some areas leave the country and shy away altogether from sharing their faith. How can you pray for Christians in lands where they are persecuted?

Verse: *"Blessed are those who are persecuted because of righteousness, for theirs is the kingdom of heaven."* (MATTHEW 5:10)

Story 42

Dying for Jesus: First Martyrs

"Greater love has no one than this, that he lay down his life for his friends." (JOHN 15:13)

I t was noontime, September 21, 1992. It seemed like any other ordinary broadcast day at DXAS, FEBC station at Tugbungan, Zamboanga City, Southwest Mindanao.

As Rev. Gregorio Hapalla, a Christian and Missionary Alliance pastor, took his place inside the studio to resume his program *Pamahon-pahun Sin Mahapun (Afternoon Reflections)* he must have felt anew a surge of energy. Stretching his limbs, he must have thought, "This is what it's all about...to reach hundreds, even thousands of my Muslim fellowmen out there, to tell them that Jesus is real. He's alive. He's Lord and Savior. Oh if they can only know the joy of such salvation!"

Zamboanga Times *article describing the incident.*

As Rev. Hapalla, 58, caught sight of Greg Bacabis, 37, DXAS chief technician, they must have exchanged a silent nod of understanding. This is it, the gesture said, the show will go on no matter what.

Such resolution must not have been easy to come by. A few weeks earlier, Rev. Hapalla had repeatedly received death threats from what they believed could have been Muslim extremists. The message was clear, "Stop talking about Jesus, or else..." But *Pamahun-pahun Sin Mahapun,* airing in Tausug for

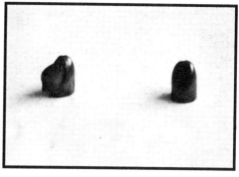

Two of the bullets that killed Rev. Greg Hapalla.

three hours on Mondays through Saturdays, was changing lives! It was gaining popularity and arming listeners with new hope and sound principles for living. What's more, FEBC's powerful transmitter is reaching areas in the Celebes Sea, over Borneo, into Indonesia. Who knows how many more listeners are coming to Jesus because of the program!

Although Rev. Hapalla went on leave shortly after the threats, he and the DXAS staff knew in their hearts that there was no way they could and would stop the broadcast. Then on September 12, Muslim leaders signed a declaration of solidarity with their Christian counterparts in the presence of President Fidel Ramos. It seemed like the start of a more lasting social peace.

1:30 p.m., September 21, 1992. A listener, Ambre Al-Hari, 27, fisherman and Sulu native, was in the studio to make a public service announcement. Then without warning, two men wielding .45 caliber pistols barged into the booth and rapidly fired at the unsuspecting occupants. The attack was so sudden that if there had been time for a split-second thought, the murdered must have simply uttered the name, "Jesus!"

Rev. Hapalla and Al-Hari died on the spot. Bacabis died at the hospital shortly after. The killers fled on a motorcycle. A month later, one was arrested and admitted responsibility. Police identified the killers as members of the Abu Sayyaf, a Muslim extremist group, the same ones who had earlier made the death threats.

The very next day, September 22, FEBC Philippines made an official statement, part of which read:

> In the midst of all the grief and trauma...we recognize that God...
> has a good purpose for allowing us to experience this tragedy...
> This causes us to affirm even more strongly our commitment to
> the Gospel ministry through radio. We also affirm our love for
> the people of Mindanao and particularly the people of Zamboanga.
> We commend Pastor Greg Hapalla and Brother Greg Bacabis to
> the Lord. Their deaths remind us all that the Christian ministry
> requires nothing less than laying our lives on the line for the Lord.

Rev. Hapalla and Brother Bacabis did not die for nothing. Today, the DXAS staff in Zamboanga carries on undaunted in spreading the good news in conflict-stricken Mindanao. Trials and persecutions may never cease, but the zeal and love of the staff for Jesus don't either.

"THE BLOOD OF THE MARTYRS IS THE SEED OF THE CHURCH" SAYS THE CHURCH FATHER TERTULLIAN. YOU AND I MUST BE WILLING TO LAY DOWN OUR LIVES FOR THE SAKE OF THE GOSPEL. IN THIS AGE OF COMPLACENCY, CONCERN FOR COMFORT AND SECURITY, WE NEED TO TAKE A CLOSER LOOK AT OUR COMMITMENT TO JESUS CHRIST. ARE WE READY TO FACE PERSECUTION OR EVEN DEATH FOR HIS SAKE?

Verse: "I tell you the truth, unless a kernel of wheat falls to the ground and dies, it remains only a single seed. But if it dies, it produces many seeds. The man who loves his life will lose it, while the man who hates his life in this world will keep it for eternal life." (JOHN 12:24-25)

Story 43

The Sword of the Spirit

"And other sheep I have which are not of this fold; them also must I bring." (JOHN 10:16)

hen FEBC co-founder Robert Bowman read this verse to the staff one morning in the early 1950's, he knew God was telling FEBC to reach heretofore unreached groups with the Gospel. A technical problem had earlier taken DZAS off the air for sometime and had driven home the point that the Gospel should not be confined to Manila and outlying areas alone. Far beyond lay the vast harvest fields of inaccessible, unreached Filipino groups. There must be a creative way to reach them. Thus, the PM "Portable Missionary" radio was born.

"Word spread across the mountains about a "box that could talk" at the seashore. One thing led to another, and after a follow-up distribution of PM's, Mangyans had soon adopted FEBC as part of their daily lives."

Conceived at a time when even radios did not come cheap, FEBC set up a workshop using assembly line methods to produce radios. The PM radios were then exclusively pre-tuned to FEBC stations and distributed to hundreds of listening outposts. With additional transmitters and expanded programming, the PM soon found its way into remote *baranggays* (villages). Two stories stand out.

For years, missionaries had tried to contact the semi-nomadic Mangyans in Mindoro but always, the natives retreated to the inner jungles. The high incidence of malaria prevented further missionary penetration. Two FEBC staff members purposely left a PM in a nipa hut along the shore. Word spread across the mountains about a "box that could talk" at the seashore. One thing led to another, and after a follow-up distribution of PM's, Mangyans soon adopted FEBC as part of their daily lives. Rev. Max Atienza's *Bukas na Aklat* was a favorite. When invited once, Rev. Atienza was treated to a one-of-a-kind worship service held in the middle of a rain forest. Not having been to a service

before, the Mangyans opened their service thus: "This is Far East Broadcasting Company, Manila"; and closed with: "Tune in again tomorrow night at this same time." Today, after much mission work by the Overseas Missionary Fellowship, the Mangyans have a good number of churches in Mindoro.

Mrs. Mercedes Sable was the only Christian in the barrio when a PM was placed in her care. The PM quickly became the talk of the town. Barrio folks soon trooped to the Sables, marveling at the contraption and eagerly listening to the Ilocano gospel programs

"Portable Missionary" set is pre tuned to DZAS.

come rain or shine. One night, pistol-wielding burglars broke into the Sables' home. While ransacking the house with the Sables at gun point, one burglar saw the PM on a cupboard. He curiously turned it on and lo, the voice of Max Atienza preaching the gospel came through loud and clear. Transfixed, the burglars listened to the entire sermon, turned the PM off afterwards, bowed to the Sables politely and backed out from the house. Five years after, FEBC's Isabelo Montejo, director of the PM department, visited the barrio. The Christians there were building a new church building and forty families had come to Christ.

GOD WORKS IN MYSTERIOUS WAYS. HE SENDS HIS PROTECTION TO HIS CHILDREN IN THE FORM OF ANGELS AND OTHER CIRCUMSTANCES TO SHIELD US FROM HARM. THE LORD HAS MADE AVAILABLE TO US SPIRITUAL WEAPONS AND FOREMOST OF THESE WEAPONS IS HIS WORD. AT THE PREACHING OF GOD'S WORD, SATAN AND EVIL SPIRITS TREMBLE. ARE YOU THANKFUL FOR THE BIBLE THAT HELPS KEEP YOU AWAY FROM EVIL AND WITHSTAND TEMPTATION?

Verse: *"Put on the full armor of God so that you can take your stand against the devil's schemes:"* - (EPHESIANS 6:11)

Story 44

Penetrating the Bamboo Curtain

*T*o the northwest of the Philippines lies the vast land of China where live over one billion people. In 1949, when Mao-Tse-Tung swung the bamboo curtain close, there were 936,000 evangelical believers. Today, conservative estimates are at over 50 million. Yet until 1978, China had been totally closed to the outside world. What happened in the intervening years? How did God make His word grow in heretofore untold proportions?

July, 1949. Two months before access to China was blocked, radio stations were being built on a safe perimeter. By the 29th of July, FEBC Philippines had begun its first broadcasts to China.

The early years. The Communist Party had early realized that in order to control such a large nation, they had to communicate to the remotest areas. Thus began a massive production of radios. By 1972, 82% of homes had at least one radio. What the Communists did for propaganda, God used for His glory— the radio became God's chief tool for evangelism and discipleship. The letters that FEBC received in these early, less restricted years confirmed that the radio signals were effective. Still, many questions were unanswered— only faith kept the broadcasts going.

1966-1976. With the Cultural Revolution came a massive crackdown on religion. The Communists burned Bibles and hymnbooks, desecrated churches, imprisoned and tortured Christians, prohibited contact with the outside world, including listening to foreign broadcasts. The press warned against "the enemy station" (FEBC) which whetted people's appetite all the more. The broadcasts went on round the clock, in six major Chinese languages, supplying Bibles through "The Bible at Dictation Speed." Letters that slipped out referred to the broadcasts as "the calling voice of God." The story is told of a Chinese Christian who showed a recent visitor to China a well-worn Bible, completely handwritten and sewn together. The Chinese man had copied it down over the years through *Liang Yu Dentai's* (or "Radio Friendship", FEBC's popular name in China) dictation program.

With the Cultural Revolution ended for two years and China beginning to open up, thousands of letters began pouring into FEBC. Stories began to unfold. By this time believers had been meeting in "house churches". The vast extent of God's work in China was becoming evident. By 1990, FEBC had received over a hundred thousand letters from every Chinese province and estimates its audience in the millions.

Dr. Donald McGavran, noted church growth authority, summed up FEBC's role in China thus: "Without doubt the majority of these new believers have come because of the broadcasts…. The whole Body of Christ owes FEBC a debt of gratitude."

GOD IS NEVER SLOW AND HIS PURPOSES ARE NEVER THWARTED SPECIALLY WHEN IT COMES TO THE BUILDING OF HIS CHURCH HERE ON EARTH. MANY IDEOLOGIES AND MOVEMENTS HAVE SOUGHT TO ANNIHILATE CHRIST'S BODY FROM THE FACE OF THE EARTH. WHAT IS ASTONISHING IS THAT IT IS IN TIMES OF PERSECUTION WHEN BELIEVERS EVEN GROW IN NUMBER. PRAISE GOD FOR HIS INSTRUMENT OF RADIO BEING USED TO TOUCH THE MOST POPULOUS NATION ON EARTH--CHINA. HOW HAVE YOU BEEN INSTRUMENTAL IN THE BUILDING UP OF THE CHURCH?

Verse: "*I will build my church, and the gates of Hades will not overcome it.*" (MATTHEW 16:18)

First Fruits

*T*he Paras family of Mindoro first listened to DZAS in 1949. Gregoria and Lope Paras came to know Jesus Christ as their personal Savior while listening to the program *Bukas Na Aklat* (The Open Book). As far as we know, they are the first persons who came to know the Lord as a result of the broadcasts.

Here's how Dr. Bob Bowman, President Emeritus of Far East Broadcasting Company, recalls the events surrounding the conversion of the Paras family:

"The first letter from the Paras family came around June 1950. It was written by one of the family who signed it as 'Miss L.A.C.' Here's what it says,

Dear Sirs: I write this letter to tell you that I am a regular listener to the station DZAS...not only me but the whole family... We are hearing different programs... These programs helped me to be near to God, and I find Christ as my personal Savior. I am praying that you may continue the broadcasting for the sake of many souls.

The day that Mr. and Mrs. Lope Paras visited Christian Radio City Manila (CRCM) was special! Their visit gave a sense of 'faith made sight,' for they were the first people to visit CRCM to tell of their new found faith in Jesus Christ. They had come from Mindoro by boat, by bus and by walking to the new radio station.

Every night they sat beside their radio listening to the Tagalog sermons and Bible studies of Max D. Atienza. Their hearts were hungry and receptive to the Word. After one year of listening they wrote that 'The spirit of Truth came upon us' (Romans 10:17). They accepted the Lord as Savior and wanted to be baptized. They invited us to come to their home.

I remember well the boat trip Max Atienza, Paul Pipkin and I took to Mindoro! The waves were high and the boat we were on was being tossed up and down... It was an exciting trip. But the most exciting part was the visit to the home of these dear people. An afternoon meeting was held and quite a large group attended. At the close of the meeting, an invitation was given and about 35 people indicated their desire to receive the Lord. And then, we all walked a little distance to a river and baptized those who desired baptism. At that particular time there were no missionaries on the Island of Mindoro."

The story continues. With his new found joy of salvation, Lope Paras began witnessing to his family and friends in Oriental Mindoro. One by one, his family came to know and love his Savior, too, and the whole barrio was affected by his witness. One of the men who came to know the Lord through this witness was a young man named Sulpicio Peñaroyo. In turn, he began to witness to others and to have a budding desire to serve the Lord. Eventually, Peñaroyo became a minister on the island of Marinduque. Today, partly as a result of his pioneering work, Marinduque has a growing community of Christians.

The first fruits of FEBC gospel programs had in turn borne fruits— fruits that remain. Sons and daughters, nephews and nieces soon followed the spiritual footsteps of Lope and Gregoria Paras. Today, many of these nephews, nieces and even grandchildren are pastors, pastors' wives or lay ministers.

HAVE YOU EVER TOSSED A PEBBLE INTO A POND AND SEEN THE RIPPLES IN THE WATER? A LIFE SAVED BY THE LORD THAT FAITHFULLY WITNESSES AND AFFECTS OTHERS IS LIKE A TINY STONE THAT CREATES RIPPLES ON THE WATER. WE ONLY NEED TO BE FAITHFUL TO OUR CALLING AND GOD WILL DO HIS PART IN BRINGING SOULS INTO HIS KINGDOM. WHO ARE THE PEOPLE IN YOUR LIFE THAT YOU NEED TO THANK FOR INTRODUCING YOU TO THE JOY OF KNOWING CHRIST?

Verse: *"Many of the Samaritans from that town believed in Him because of the woman's testimony... they said to the woman, 'We no longer believe just because of what you said; now we have heard for ourselves, and we know that this Man really is the Savior of the world'"* (JOHN 4:39,42)

Don't Do it!

S he seized a kitchen knife intending to kill herself. Then her six-month old baby cried and she came to her senses. She realized what a great sin it would have been to take her own life. At that moment, a Scripture verse she heard long ago flashed through her mind, "For God so loved the world that He gave His only begotten Son..."

What could drive a woman to such despair that she would attempt to commit suicide? For Liza, it was the unfaithfulness of her husband.

Liza thought she and her husband were doing great. They had been happy together for several years and had one child they both loved very much. She thought that nothing that could mar their sweet life together. She felt secure in her husband's love.

Imagine Liza's shock, therefore, when in July 1997, her husband confessed to her that he had had an affair with another woman. Although the brief relationship was not serious, this hurt her terribly. She felt cheated and betrayed by her husband whom she trusted implicitly.

Rage, hatred and desire for revenge filled her heart every time she would see her husband. Her agony was aggravated by the fact that despite her pain, she did not want to destroy her husband's reputation so she could not talk to anyone about her problem.

> *"What could drive a woman to such despair that she would attempt to commit suicide? For Liza, it was the unfaithfulness of her husband."*

She became deeply depressed. In her depression she heard urgings within her telling her to separate from her husband. Or take revenge. Or better yet, the tempter inside whispered, why don't you just end your misery by killing yourself?

That was when she grabbed a kitchen knife to commit suicide. Thankfully she was saved by the cry of her baby and the reminder of a Scripture verse. She cried her heart out to God. "Forgive me for what I meant to do. But why me? Why have you given this terrible pain to me? Please remove this pain and rage in my heart. What should I do?"

Then she thought of listening to the radio and it so happened that when she turned on the radio the dial was on 702 DZAS. The counseling program "Heartline" was on air. She listened to the counsel given to callers who were going through the same problem she was struggling with. She came to realize she was not the only one with a problem, that there were those whose problems were even greater than her own.

As she continued to listen she came to understand what it really meant to be a Christian. She prayed with the counselor, Pastor Willy Basilio, and accepted Christ as her own Lord and Saviour. She also realized that God had not forsaken her, that He, in fact, loved her and redeemed her with His blood. This decision gave her the comfort she needed and the power to forgive.

Later, Liza talked to her husband. "I love you very much," she told him, "and no matter what happens I will always love you. I forgive you."   Her husband promised her he will never be unfaithful again.

They have since then invited a third person in their relationship, Jesus Christ. They now go to church together, pray together and live in peace, love and harmony. And, Liza adds, they continue to listen avidly to DZAS because they learn a lot about how to grow in their spiritual lives and how to live as a Christian in this world.

✿ YOU ONLY NEED TO LOOK A LITTLE FARTHER TO SEE THAT PEOPLE AROUND YOU ARE HURTING. THERE ARE TIMES YOU FEEL OVERWHELMED BY YOUR OWN PROBLEMS BUT REMEMBER THAT THERE ARE STILL THOSE WHO HAVE BIGGER TRIALS AND NEED THE HELP AND HOPE YOU CAN OFFER IN CHRIST. AS A CHRISTIAN YOU HAVE RESOURCES THAT A NON-BELIEVER DOESN'T: PRAYER, THE WORD OF GOD AND THE FELLOWSHIP OF BELIEVERS. ARE YOU REACHING OUT TO OTHERS USING THE RESOURCES GOD HAS ENTRUSTED TO YOU?

Verse: *"Carry each other's burdens, and in this you will fulfill the law of Christ."* (GALATIANS 6:2)

Story 47

Called to the Ministry

*I*n the early 60's, Dr. Bob Bowman, President of Far East Broadcasting Company at the time, visited England. After one of Dr. Bowman's meetings in London, a young Englishman introduced himself as a student of London Bible College studying for the ministry as a result of FEBC broadcasts. This statement puzzled Dr. Bowman because, although FEBC broadcasts in the short wave band and received some mail from listeners in Western Europe, England was not part of its primary target area.

The Englishman's explanation unfolded an awesome story that showed how God had used radio in a remote jungle to reach out to a man He had claimed for eternity and marked for His service.

The Englishman was doing government work in Borneo and was living far from God. He was sent to work among head-hunter tribes in a remote jungle village several days' journey from civilization. When he arrived in the village, the tribespeople started to treat him like a god. It seemed that his blond looks and Anglo-Saxon name were so similar to those of their heathen god that they believed a descendant of this god had come to live with them. In superstitious awe, the tribesmen began to worship him.

"When he arrived in the village, the tribespeople started to treat him like a god."

At first, he was amused by the homage but as boredom set in, he started to encourage the practice.

However, his Australian companion who was helping him in the work was overwhelmed by the strangeness of their jungle life and the primitive conditions they had to cope with. The extreme loneliness began to affect this Australian until he lost his reason. He became so violent that the Englishman had to tie him in a boat and travel five days by river out to civilization to seek medical help.

When he returned to his outpost alone, the experience left him sober and shaken. It was then that he started to listen to a little transistor radio owned by the village chief. While tuning across the dial, the student found the station of Far East Broadcasting Company and began to listen regularly.

How did transistor radio receivers get in such a remote jungle village? Apparently, Chinese traders came up the village once a year to collect rubber the tribespeople had gathered during the year and then paid them with transistor radios.

As our student listened to the FEBC broadcasts night after night, he encountered the Lord Jesus Christ and his whole life was changed. It was soon after that that he went back to England and studied at the Bible college to prepare for the ministry. When Dr. Bowman returned to England in 1965, he met this young man again. At this time, he was now pastoring a church and joyfully serving the Lord.

WHEN THE LORD EXTENDS HIS GRACE TO A SINNER, HE DOES IT OUT OF HIS ABUNDANT LOVE AND MERCY. SUCH LOVE WE CANNOT COMPREHEND. CHRIST'S LOVE FOR US IS UNCONDITIONAL, WITH NO STRINGS ATTACHED. AND ONCE WE'RE CAPTURED BY IT, WE CANNOT HELP BUT RESPOND BY GIVING OUR LIVES TO SERVE HIM. IN WHAT WAYS ARE YOU RESPONDING TO GOD'S LOVE IN YOUR LIFE?

Verse: *"For Christ's love compels us…and He died for all, that all who live should no longer live for themselves but for Him who died for them and was raised again"* -(2 CORINTHIANS 5:14-15).

Marked for God

$\mathcal{E}$very now and then, God grabs a man and literally brings him to the end of his wits to drive home a point. Such was the dramatic encounter Fred Magbanua had with his Maker.

Fred grew up in Negros where, though reared in the traditional Philippine religion, he never had a personal relationship with Christ. Then, as a young boy during World War II, he saw fear and death everywhere. After the war, he began listening to FEBC's broadcasts and in 1949, surrendered his life fully to Christ.

Though wanting to go to Bible school, Fred studied civil engineering to help his family financially. Still, determined to serve his Savior, he joined an itinerant evangelistic team. It was then that he met his future bride and ministry partner, Aliw. Spiritually mature beyond her years, Aliw had determined to serve the Lord. After they married, Fred pastored a small church but, soon realizing that he needed more training, enrolled in the Far Eastern Bible Institute. The school happened to be next door to FEBC's Manila station and Fred began working as an engineer and broadcaster for FEBC.

Temptation came, as it usually does, in a subtle form. A letter from an old classmate in the U.S. came urging Fred to accept a high-paying engineering job. Aliw was not impressed and reminded Fred of his promise never to take a job not connected with spreading the gospel. That night, while recording his program at the station, Fred decided to accept the job anyway. He rationalized that he could support FEBC and pastors with the extra money he would earn.

What happened next jolted him out of his illusions. On his way out, he noticed that the top light on the 308-foot DZAS tower was out. Fred climbed the tower to replace the light. When he reached the top, he got too close to the high voltage antenna. Instantly, radio frequency (RF) current reached out and grabbed his hair and literally for a few seconds, Fred hung by his hair 308 feet above the ground! Just then, he heard his own program, which he had recorded earlier and his own voice coming through his skull: "I beseech you, therefore, brethren, by the mercies of God that you present your bodies as a living sacrifice..." (Romans 12:1). At that moment, Fred seemed to hear the Lord say "Fred, you were telling others to surrender their lives to me, but you yourself were trying to run away to New York to better yourself."

A fuse blew, releasing Fred. A leg caught on a brace saved him from a deathly fall. His head severely burned, Fred was rushed to the hospital after he was able to miraculously make his way to the compound nurse's home. Hundreds prayed for him and three months after, the x-rays showed no brain damage.

Rev. Fred Magbanua went on to become FEBC-Philippines Managing Director for more than 20 years. Today, retired from FEBC, he remains faithful in serving the Lord. He still bears the scars from where the electricity hit him. But more than those he bears the lasting imprint of God's calling in his life.

WHEN WE ARE TEMPTED TO QUIT THE RACE THAT HAS BEEN SET BEFORE US, GOD MORE OFTEN THAN NOT, SENDS US REMINDERS THAT WE BELONG TO HIM. HE LETS US KNOW THAT HE HAS A PLAN FOR US AND HE ISN'T FINISHED WITH US YET. WHAT ARE THE REMINDERS THAT GOD IS BRINGING INTO YOUR LIFE TO STRENGTHEN YOU IN THE RACE THAT HE HAS SET BEFORE YOU?

Verse: "...And let us run with perseverance the race marked out for us. Let us fix our eyes on Jesus, the author and perfector of our faith."
(HEBREWS 12:1-2)

Story 49

Real Riches in Christ

*M*arilou was born the youngest of eight children to parents enjoying a high status in society. From the time she was born, though, she knew rejection. For unknown reasons, she stayed in the hospital until she was a year old. She would have been adopted by a childless couple had her brothers and sisters not insisted on keeping her. So she stayed with her grandparents and for most of her childhood, she shuffled back and forth between household with contrasting lifestyles : one was simple, reserved and rigidly religious but severely lacking in affection; the other was marked by luxury and social status which only masked the physical beatings, hostility and ridicule suffered by the children.

> *"Very quickly the romance turned into a nightmare. The man Marilou had chosen turned out to be physically and verbally abusive, had a vile temper and was clinging to his mother. "*

The children grew up with hardened hearts as they tried to cope in a dysfunctional family. But the years took their toll: in their teens, two siblings eloped; others were sent to relatives for care and Marilou was expelled from a boarding school. The tide seemed to turn when at 18, Marilou won the title of Miss Young Philippines at the Bb. Pilipinas 1976 Beauty Pageant. For a year, she enjoyed the prestige and attention along with the responsibility.

Then she met a man — brilliant, eloquent, nine years her senior and fresh out of jail. After a whirlwind courtship, she eloped with him despite family objections. Before her turn was up as a title holder, she was six months pregnant.

Very quickly the romance turned into a nightmare. The man Marilou had chosen turned out to be physically and verbally abusive, had a vile

Marilou

temper and was clinging to his mother. Despite all difficulties, Marilou strove to meet the demands of being wife and mother. At times, she had to suppress the seed of hostility she grew up with and refrain from turning child discipline into beatings.

Through the years, she and her husband continued to grow apart. When the family moved to the U.S. in 1991, Marilou thought the situation would improve. But by then, they had become completely emotionally estranged. Marilou coped by drowning herself in work, family, children and seven dogs. Finally, the marriage broke down in 1995.

Left with no home, no children, no job and facing court battles, Marilou became bitter, lonely and angry. All the fears of her childhood resurfaced and through it all, she questioned God's presence while crying out at the same time for help.

God answered. When Marilou returned to Manila, she met friends who knew Jesus. One led her in prayer and in October 1996, she received Jesus as her Savior and Lord. Then her brother pointed her to FEBC's DZAS. Soon, listening became part of her daily routine. Listening to programs such as **Heartline**, *Hardin ng Panalangin*, **In Touch, Back to the Bible, Grace to You, Day by Day** and **Insight for Living**, Marilou received spiritual feeding and practical insights. At one point, she resolved to write her husband, asking for and giving forgiveness. Inspired by a program she listened to, she simply shared her testimony and the workings of God in her life. As she is ministered to, so is Marilou able to minister to those who go through the same pains she did.

Today, Marilou is active in her local church. Her spiritual preparation enables her not only to live on, but to stand victorious in daily spiritual warfare.

✿ OUR LIFE IS LIKE WET CLAY IN THE POTTER'S HANDS. BEFORE WE MET CHRIST, WE WERE A VESSEL UNFIT, UNCLEAN AND USED IN A DISHONORABLE MANNER. BUT THERE IS HOPE BECAUSE WE CAN BE MOLDED AND RESHAPED BY OUR LORD FOR HIS DESIGN AND PURPOSES AS WE ARE WILLING TO YIELD OURSELVES TO HIS HANDS. HOW THANKFUL WE WILL BE FOR HIS WORKING IN OUR LIVES. IN WHAT WAYS IS GOD SHAPING YOUR CHARACTER?

Verse: *"Yet, O Lord, You are our Father, we are the clay, you are the Potter; we are all the work of your hand".* (ISAIAH 64:8)

God's Hand in Philippine History

Story **50**

*W*hat should Christians do when, as citizens, they are called to participate in civil disobedience against a widely perceived dishonest government? What is the role of Christian radio in such circumstance?

FEBC Philippines got the chance to find answers to these questions in the laboratory of real life during the Philippine "EDSA Revolution" of 1986.

On February 7, 1986 a most eventful election with the presidential seat hotly contested between then President Ferdinand Marcos and opposition candidate Cory Aquino was held nationwide. FEBC extensively covered the event for 17 hours in "Decision '86."

February 15. The Philippine Parliament declared President Marcos winner. The next day, Mrs. Aquino called for a nationwide protest with a seven-point program of non-violent "civil disobedience" actions. The program had promise of gaining popular acceptance.

February 20. The Christian Leaders Alliance of the Philippines, a group of evangelical leaders headed by Rev. Fred Magbanua (then FEBC Managing Director) decided to respond relevantly and Biblically to the pressing issues by holding several marathon broadcasts on DZAS and DZFE-FM.

February 22, Saturday. The first marathon broadcast went on air from 8:00 a.m. to 2:00 p.m. The numerous phone calls indicated that, indeed, there was a need to address the issues of civil disobedience and present Biblical views on government. That very evening, FEBC heard that Defense Minister Juan Ponce Enrile and Armed Forces Chief of Staff Gen. Fidel Ramos had withdrawn allegiance to Marcos and were calling the rest of the military to join the "New Armed Forces of the People." A *coup d'etat* was in the offing.

Rev. Magbanua and then Domestic Operations Manager Efren Pallorina quickly decided to go back on the air with "Decision '86." In the midst of all the events quickly unfolding and the uncertainty of their outcome, FEBC determined that two things were to mark its coverage: prayer and Bible readings. Many people glued to their radio sets were praying fervently for the whole situation.

> *In the midst of all the events quickly unfolding and the uncertainty of their outcome, FEBC determined that two things were to mark its coverage: prayer and Bible readings.*

11:00 p.m. FEBC's first mobile team was already at the action scene between Camps Aguinaldo and Crame to report on the crowd gathering to form a human barricade against Marcos' troops.

February 23, Sunday. The human barricade swelled. All day long, FEBC advised Christian callers to seek their consciences on whether or not to be a part of "People Power." Those who did join were encouraged to bring banners with Bible verses to remind people of God's sovereignty.

February 25. FEBC aired "live" the inauguration of Cory Aquino at Club Filipino, as well as that of Ferdinand Marcos at Malacañang Palace. 10:00 p.m. After much verification of rumors, FEBC finally released the story that the Marcos and Ver families had left Malacañang Palace for the United States. The crisis was over! On the air, the hosts along with Director Magbanua, Pastor Proceso Marcelo and FEBC Chaplain Dale Golding joined the nation in giving thanks to God who remains sovereign over the affairs of a nation.

February 26, 5:30 a.m. "Decision '86" wrapped up after the team members shared the profound impact the coverage had on them. The hard work—from making coffee, washing dishes and emptying waste baskets to answering phones, monitoring radio stations and sending out coverage teams—was a once-in-a-lifetime experience and well worth it.

So what is the role of Christian radio in a national crisis? To lead people in prayer, Biblical perspectives and the acknowledgement that in good times or bad, God is Lord of all!

NO CREDIT SHOULD BE GIVEN TO ANYONE EXCEPT TO THE LORD JESUS CHRIST FOR THE "PEOPLE POWER REVOLUTION" IN THE PHILIPPINES. WHEN GOD HAS A PLAN FOR A NATION, HE WORKS THROUGH ITS PEOPLE AND ITS LEADERS. HE CAN CHANGE THE HEART OF ANY PERSON. INDEED OUR GOD IS SOVEREIGN AND CONTINUES TO ORCHESTRATE HIS WILL FOR EVERY PEOPLE IN EVERY NATION INCLUDING THE PHILIPPINES. IN WHAT WAYS CAN YOU SEE GOD'S HAND THROUGHOUT OUR NATION'S HISTORY?

Verse: *"If My people who are called by My name, will humble themselves and pray and seek My face and turn from their wicked ways, then I will hear from heaven and will forgive their sin and will heal their land."*

(2 CHRONICLES 7:14)

Appendices

Stones of Remembrance

he date was July 6, 1946, only one year after the end of World War II. John Broger walked off the *SS Lane Victory* on Manila Bay into a city which still bore the scars of battle. After seeing the spiritual needs of Asia, he and Robert Bowman were burdened by God to initiate Christian radio broadcasts to all of Asia.

He had just come from China where he had applied for a radio franchise but there had been no response. Now, because the ship stopped in Manila, he decided to try here.

At this time, Far East Broadcasting Company was newly incorporated in the United States and had no radio stations anywhere. John started at once to set up a Filipino subsidiary of FEBC. With the help of Attorney Leon O. Ty, he obtained the papers necessary for applying for radio stations. The incorporators were Atty Leon O. Ty, John Broger, Tirso Joson, Filemon Salcedo and Santiago Cruspero.

When Broger submitted the application to the Ministry of Communications they still contained some blank spaces. He didn't have answers for the following: how FEBC will be financed; the amount of power they will be using, and the location of the proposed transmitter site. The application could not be processed unless all questions were answered.

John left the office with some discouragement. After much prayer for God's direction he returned with the new application. Those three blanks remained.

"Where will your funding come from?" came the first question. "Sir, we have faith in God to meet our needs," John answered.

"Faith! What do you mean?"

"We believe God will supply all the money to build this station and keep it on the air. We will not be receiving any money through advertising. God will supply our needs," John replied and then quoted Hebrews 11:1. "Faith is the substance of things hoped for, the evidence of things not seen."

"Well," replied the man, "I don't understand that kind of faith but if you think you can manage on that, we'll give you a try. Now, about the power, how much?"

"Ten thousand watts," John said quickly and watched as that number was penciled in.

"Where will your equipment be located?" was the next question.

"Could I have two days on that question?" asked John.

Six weeks later he still had not found a suitable place. One day a letter arrived from the Ministry of Communications. Mr. Broger quickly tore open the bulky envelop. There was the franchise stamped "APPROVED" with the provision that the site be named as soon as possible. But something was different. Where he had seen the words "ten thousand watts" penciled in, someone had crossed them out and had written in large letters "UNLIMITED POWER!"

This first franchise was really the birth certificate of FEBC Philippines, executed by an unknown hand. Only God knew what He was planning here. Only He knew the need for unlimited power.

Today, just as Joshua commanded the Israelites to bring stones from the Jordan River bed, to be piled up as a reminder of God's miracle crossing of that river, let us lay a Stone of Remembrance in memory of this event. God set the parameters of this ministry. Let future generations never forget that God chose the Philippines and marked out the boundaries with His own hand. This first stone is for God's intervention in this project's birth.

After obtaining permission to operate, FEBC had to show proof of performance. They were given a deadline to go on the air. John Broger and his men worked long hours day and night to build the transmitter building, install the transmitter and get ready to broadcast. Through a series of miracles and God's timely provision, they finally went on air on June 4, 1948. Over KZAS, a 1,000-watt transmitter, the majestic strains of "All Hail the Power of Jesus' Name" ushered in the maiden broadcast of FEBC.

Let's lay another Stone of Remembrance for this event when, through God's miraculous intervention, the Gospel first went on air from the first station of FEBC. Let this stone remind us of all the other stations that went on the air. Seven short wave stations for reaching all of Asia, and nine local stations for broadcasting to Metro Manila and throughout the islands of the Philippines.

This first small transmitter had only two poles with a wire strung between them as its antenna. But soon a 10,000 watt transmitter arrived and was installed. Now another need became urgent; a tower to make the signal heard. Prayer was made daily.

One day a company executive telephoned Bob Bowman. They had heard that FEBC was looking for a tower. His company had ordered three towers but needed only two. He was offering the third tower to Bob for over $6,000, a great savings from the original price of $25,000. When Bob said FEBC didn't have that kind of money, the caller asked about FEBC, its mission, how it was financed. He had trouble understanding about faith. Then he asked how much FEBC would be willing to pay. Bob sheepishly answered, "We have about $300 in the bank." The man promised to call him back.

The next afternoon the same man telephoned Bowman and said his company had agreed to the price of $300! The wood crating material holding the pieces together would have cost far more than $300.

Let us lay a Stone of Remembrance for this and all the equipment that God has provided throughout the years. It is a monument to God's deep interest in this radio project and His unlimited ability to answer prayers. Since then He has continued to provide the hardware that gives voice to the Gospel in Asia, including a brand new 50 kilowatt transmitter to replace the World War II vintage DZAS transmitter dedicated in 1997. Let each generation be reminded by this stone, that God has provided in amazing ways year after year, upgrading and updating our facilities until we have all that we see today.

By 1949, FEBC started broadcasting to China, that vast country of teeming millions. One of the first Chinese broadcasters was Mrs. Phoebe Chua. She was a tireless broadcaster who helped the ministry in many ways until her old age. Let's add a Stone of Remembrance for the first Chinese broadcast, to commemorate our founders' vision to reach people groups in their heart language. This stone will also remind us of all the languages that have been added to our schedule: more than 60 Asian languages and more than 20 Philippine languages and dialects.

In 1995, two missionaries in Thailand took video clips of tribal communities in the mountains of Thailand and Vietnam who listened to our Hmong broadcasts. Whole villages have turned to the Lord from their animistic practice as a result of the broadcasts.

Let us lay a Stone of Remembrance for the Hmongs who were moved from darkness to light because of the Gospel they heard on their radios. Let this remind us of the countless people whose lives have been touched by God through our programs. Whole tribes coming to Christ. The Degas in Vietnam. The Dumagats in Luzon. Men in prison finding spiritual freedom. People on the verge of suicide finding new lease in life. Let us not forget that God who commanded us to preach the gospel to people groups have also enabled us to do so.

People are God's greatest gift to FEBC Philippines. He continues to call workers from all over the world to band together in this great work. Together with the workers and missionaries are the thousands of partners who pray for the ministry and give financial support. People like you. Let's lay a Stone of Remembrance to remind us that God is the Lord of the Harvest and He calls His workers from wherever He chooses to do tasks He assigns them to do...whether it be doing front line duty or being a support to those in the front line.

There are countless other stones that could be laid, in memory of the Portable Missionaries, pre-tuned radios that met an early need; of unbelievable financial provisions, of the "ordination" of Fred Magbanua on top of the DZAS tower, the sacrifices offered by Byrd Brunemeier and the two Gregs who died in the line of duty. But we will have to wait for eternity to have time to tell them all.

These Stones of Remembrance remind us that God's hand has set the parameters of this work. God has provided the men and women, machines, money and methods. God has sheltered us through every danger. As Joshua said to the children of Israel in his day, "He did this so that all people of the earth might know that the hand of the LORD is powerful and so that you might always fear the Lord your God." Joshua 4:24

To God be the Glory!

- Belvah Golding

DZAS Radio Station
License obtained in 1948

Different Languages
Being Aired from FEBC

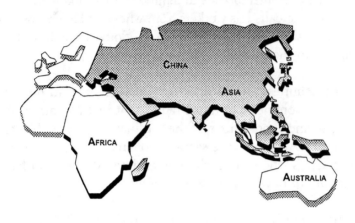

Atsi	Amoy	Jeh	Lao
Bama Burmese	Cantonese	Jorai	Malay
Chin-Asho	Mandarin	Katu	Mien
Chin-Haka	Swatow	Koho	Bicolano
Chin-Khumi	Zhuang	Mnong	Bilaan
Chin Tidin	Aceh	Muong	Cebuano
Kachin-Jingpo	Indonesian	Nung	Chavacano
Kachin-Lisu	Javanese	Raday	Ilocano
Lahu	Minangkabau	Rengao	Ilonggo
Chin-Lushai	Sasak	Roglai	Manobo
Maru	Sundanese	Sedang	Matigsalog
Nagau-Makwere	Batak	Tho	Sambal Botolan
Palaung-Pale	Ogan	White Thai	Sambal Tina
Kachin-Rawang	Komering	Vietnamese	Tagalog
Shan	English	Ao-Naga	T'boli
Wa	Bahnar	Kuki	Leyteño
Daai-Chin	Black Thai	Mei-Tei	Yakan
Mon	Bru	Zoukam	
Karen-Po	Chrau	Akha	
Karen-Thai	Chru	White Hmong	
(Sgaw)	Eastern Cham	Blue Hmong	
Khmer	Hre	Khmu	

FEBC Philippine
Radio Coverage

FEBC Philippines Stations

Luzon
DZAS / Manila 702 AM
DZFE / Manila 98.7 FM
DWRF / Local / Iba 1458 AM
DWAS / Legaspi 1125 AM

Visayas
DYVS / Bacolod City   1233 AM
DYFR-FM / Cebu City 98.7 FM

Mindanao
DXFE / Davao City 1197 AM
DXKI / Marbel 1062 AM
DXAS / Zamboanga 1116 AM

OTHER BROADCASTS
Pagpamalandong
DYVL 819 9:30 PM (Monday - Saturday)
(Leyteño Broadcast on Commercial Station)

Kumusta Po Kabayan?
(Tagalog Program for Filipino workers
in Middle East)
15.540 mHz
19 meter band, 1000-1100 GMT
Fridays
15.555 mHz
19 meter band 0500 GMT
Sundays

International Services
Seven transmitters covering China, India and
Southeast Asia in 64 languages and dialects.

Acknowledgements

EDITORIAL STAFF:
Eden Faith Baldemor, Petite Calica, Ichet Lacsina, Suzette Peña,
and the staff of DXAS Zamboanga and DYFR Cebu

TYPING AND PROOFREADING:
Elenita Angeles, Arleen Cena, Rowie Hizon

PHOTOS:
Fernando Roxas, Ronnel Rubrica, Raquel Landong, DXAS Zamboanga,
FEBC La Mirada, Marinus Landman

DESIGN AND PRINTING:
Maldwyn de Pano (Design Plus)

STORIES WERE CONDENSED AND ADAPTED FROM:
- *The Signal* (FEBC Philippines Publication)
- *The Broadcaster* (FEBC La Mirada, California)
- Bowman, Eleanor. **Eyes Beyond the Horizon.**
Tennessee: Thomas Nelson Inc. (1991)
- Bowman, Jim (Ed.). FEBC *International Newsletter*
(April 1997 and Summer 1996) FEBC: La Mirada, California
- Ledyard, Gleason. **Skywaves.** Chicago: Moody Press (1963).
- Actual Letters and interviews

PERMISSION TO REPRINT THE FOLLOWING ARTICLES:
- "Basilio Clark" - Taken from Heroes: People Who
Made A Difference in Our World, ©1997
by Harold Sala and published in the Philippines by OMF Literature Inc.
- "Questions I Had No Answer For" (Reynald Malinao)
- Taken from Resources For the Blind Newsletter
(January 1996) by Dr. Randy Weisser
- "I've Found the Ultimate Reality" - by Oscar Emmanuel Cruz
as told to Willie Marquez, Alliance Publishers, Inc. (1979)

More Precious
 Gthan old

I was blessed by the stories in this book and would like to invest in that which is "more precious than Gold" - the lives of unreached people in the Philippines and the rest of Asia. I want to challenge them with the radio messages of the saving knowledge of Jesus Christ.

NAME: _____

ADDRESS: _____

_____

TELEPHONE: _____

❏ I would like to share a one-time love gift of:
P/$ _____
❏ I would like to support the ministry on a regular basis: P/$ _____ every _____
❏ I would like to be placed on your mailing list to receive material for prayer and information.
❏ I would like to order _____ copies of this book.

Please do not send cash by mail. Send crossed-check or money order to Far East Broadcasting Company by registered mail to P.O. Box 1, 0560 Valenzuela City, Philippines. FEBC is a registered donee institution. Tels. 292-5603 • Fax no. 291-4982 • E-mail dev@febc.org.ph